Mondays with Mary

A Celebration of Marian Feasts Throughout the Year

Mondays with Mary

A Celebration of Marian Feasts Throughout the Year

Meredith Henning

Second Edition

Mondays with Mary:
A Celebration of Marian Feast Throughout the Year
Second Edition

Cover design by Ted Schluenderfritz
Our Lady of Good Counsel illustration by Sean Fitzpatrick
All other Marian illustrations by Cliff Vasko
Floral images from *Decorative Floral Designs* (Mineola, NY: Dover, 2003),
used by permission
Except Forget-me-not and Venus Looking Glass by Cliff Vasko

All scripture references come from Douay-Rheims Bible (New York, Abradale Press, 1959).

Any omission of credits is unintentional. The author/publisher requests documentation for future printings.

Special note for the second edition: The illustrations as well as the recipe cards in Appendix F may be photocopied for your personal use only. We encourage you to use the illustrations at the beginning of each section as well as the images of flowers throughout the book as coloring pages for your teatime activity. We sized them small for use by small hands. They can be glued to cardstock and used in your projects.

Litany of Loreto

Lord, have mercy on us.
Christ have mercy on us.
Lord, have mercy on us.
Christ, hear us.
Christ graciously hear us.
God, the Father of heaven, have mercy on us.
God the Son, Redeemer of the world, have mercy on us.
God the Holy Ghost, have mercy on us.
Holy Trinity, one God, have mercy on us.

Holy Mary, pray for us.
Holy Mother of God, . . .
Holy Virgin of virgins, . . .
Mother of Christ, . . .
Mother of divine grace, . . .
Mother most pure, . . .
Mother most chaste, . . .
Mother inviolate, . . .
Mother undefiled, . . .
Mother most amiable, . . .
Mother most admirable, . . .
Mother of good counsel, . . .
Mother of our Creator, . . .
Mother of our Savior, . . .
Virgin most prudent, . . .
Virgin most venerable, . . .
Virgin most renowned, . . .
Virgin most powerful, . . .
Virgin most merciful, . . .
Virgin most faithful, . . .
Mirror of justice, . . .
Seat of wisdom, . . .
Cause of our joy, . . .
Spiritual vessel, . . .
Vessel of honor, . . .
Singular vessel of devotion, . . .
Mystical Rose, . . .
Tower of David, . . .
Tower of ivory, . . .
House of gold, . . .
Ark of the covenant, . . .
Gate of heaven, . . .
Morning star, . . .

Health of the sick, . . .
Refuge of sinners, . . .
Comforter of the afflicted, . . .
Help of Christians, . . .
Queen of Angels, . . .
Queen of Patriarchs, . . .
Queen of Prophets, . . .
Queen of Apostles, . . .
Queen of Martyrs, . . .
Queen of Confessors, . . .
Queen of Virgins, . . .
Queen of all Saints, . . .
Queen conceived without original sin, . .
Queen assumed into heaven, . . .
Queen of the most holy Rosary, . . .
Queen of Peace, pray for us.

Lamb of God, who takest away the sins of the world, spare us, O Lord.
Lamb of God, who takest away the sins of the world, graciously hear us O Lord.
Lamb of God, who takest away the sins of the world, have mercy on us.

V. Pray for us, O holy Mother of God.
R. That we may be made worthy of the promises of Christ.

Let us pray.
Grant, we beseech Thee, O Lord God, unto us Thy servants, that we may rejoice in continual health of mind and body; and, by the glorious intercession of Blessed Mary ever Virgin, may be delivered from present sadness, and enter into the joy of Thine eternal gladness. Through Christ our Lord. Amen.

To the Blessed Mother in all her glorious titles . . .

"I know there seems to be neither order nor sense in what I write, but because I long so dearly to possess You, I am looking for You everywhere, like Solomon, wandering in all directions (Wisdom 8:18). If I am striving to make You known in this world, it is because You Yourself have promised that all who explain You and make You known will have eternal life (cf. Sirach 8:18). Accept, then, my loving Lord, these humble words of mine as though they were a masterly discourse. Look upon the strokes of my pen as so many steps to find You and from Your throne above bestow Your blessings and Your enlightenment on what I mean to say about You, so that those who read it may be filled with a fresh desire to love You and possess You, on earth as well as in heaven."

—Saint Louis de Montfort (*The Love of Eternal Wisdom*, Montfort Missionaries, 1987)

Church in village of Montfort-sur-Meu (photo courtesy Julia Fogassy)

Acknowledgments

This book would not have been possible without the loving support of my family. I especially want to thank my dear sweet husband without whom I could never have dreamed up this reality and for all his love and guidance in the wee dark hours of writing!

Mondays with Mary might not have come to fruition if I wasn't presenting and sharing all of these ideas first and foremost with my incredible children, Emma, Benjamin, Elijah and Gabriel. I am grateful to be their mother and to be able to teach them about Our Heavenly Mother at home.

I also wish to acknowledge:

My dear parents, without whom, I would not be here.

Meredith Gould, my new friend and advisor, and author of many wonderful Catholic books. She has been an enthusiastic writing coach, editor and full-fledged first name sharer!

Julia Fogassy, for letting me pick her brain constantly about the process and graciously letting me share in her knowledge of writing for home schoolers.

Kathleen Lawson, my incredible friend and confidante. I thank her for her encouragement and constant friendship, even after all these years.

May we always go to Jesus through Mary!

Table of Contents

PLEASE NOTE: Devotional activities are presented in the book in the order of the *Litany of Loreto* (see page 5). For a list of the activities keyed to the calendar, please see Appendix E.

Introduction

The Invitation

When we first began Mondays with Mary, I was elated to discover such a joyous, engaged response from my children about our new "Mary" time. While this was not their first exposure to Marian devotions, my previous approach (during school time) was not only met with boredom, but led to discouragement on my part. Mary, I realized, is not someone to "learn" about, she is someone to yearn for. She is not a project to be finished and then put away, she is a cherished gift from God; a refuge for us to return to again and again. She is Our Heavenly Mother.

We had always prayed the family rosary in the evening; we had prayed litanies, novenas, and carried out many May coronations. We marveled at the birth of Our Lord and at the *fiat* of his Mother, but we needed more. *I needed more.* What better way for a Catholic mother of four to instill our rich faith and most especially a faithful devotion to Our Blessed Mother than with a special focused devotion time? What better way to reach Jesus than through His ever-Virgin and faithful Mother? This was it! And so *Mondays with Mary* was born.

Mondays with Mary represents a glimpse into the life and heart of the Blessed Virgin Mary for our children. We as their parents are the windows to her world; we just need to open it for them. Let us go to Jesus through Mary!

The Inspiration

The inspiration for this book came one day as I pondered the *Litany of Loreto*. I was struck by the symbolism and joy of this litany and how it represents every aspect of Our Lady's life as a free, loving gift to the world. Dating back to the fourteenth century, the *Litany of Loreto* includes almost every reality of Mary we celebrate.

At the time, I had been receiving some beautiful novena notifications via email from one of my dearest friends, Alice Gunther, author of *Haystack Full of Needles: A Catholic Home Educator's Guide to Socialization* (Pennsylvania, Hillside Education, 2008). I received each message with joy, knowing I would be able to pray for a person in our online community and that Mary was taking all our prayers and devotions straight to Our Heavenly Father. This was so very meaningful and real for me that I wanted to share this practice with my dear children. Our Catholic faith is so rich in tradition and symbolism that I wanted the *Litany of Loreto* to be a tradition-building tool that would create memories of our times together with Mother Mary.

For the past few years I have shared the content and activities of our *Mondays with Mary* through posts on my home education blog—*Sweetness and Light.* Because of the heartfelt joy and positive response from my readership, I felt called to put it into a book format so others could benefit from this Marian devotion and the many graces that flowed into our family as a result.

It is my deep desire that this book will enrich your life and bestow upon your family the grace of Our Lady and her Son, Jesus Christ. This is what *Mondays with Mary* is all about!

The Implementation

How then might we more fully appreciate all of Our Blessed Mother's feasts and apparitions? I have found that the *Litany of Loreto* provides a framework for celebrating Marian feasts throughout the liturgical year. I hope you will discover how using the *Litany* for hands-on devotion provides a powerfully effective focus for teaching your dear children about their heavenly Mother and making her seem more real to them — and you.

Each title found in the *Litany of Loreto* helps us to explore an aspect of Mary's life that the Church reverences and I have provided practical suggestions for celebrating at home. These suggestions include devotional activities, teatime recipe ideas, and other ways to remember Our Lady and her worthiness for feasting and celebrating! There are also some appendices at the back for you to peruse.

The format for this book is simple, straightforward, and can be expanded to include your own family customs and traditions. Because each feast is self-contained and none is a prerequisite for another, you can celebrate them all within each liturgical year cycle, or select the ones that are most convenient and special to your group or family and plan accordingly. The book is designed to be used each year, so it is just fine to pick and choose what suits your family.

Here are some suggestions to help you prepare. I offer the following as a blueprint for planning ahead for your Mondays with Mary, and to generate wonder and anticipation in your children. Although this book was developed mainly for home use, it would also work well for any small gathering within or outside your parish. If you travel this route, feel free to delegate some of the preparation. Perhaps one family could bring teatime treats; another could bring beverages or craft supplies. Make it work for you in a simple and relaxed manner. Your focus, after all, is celebrating a feast in honor of Mary!

On your very first *Mondays with Mary*, prepare your environment with these essential elements:

1. **Make a Marian space reflecting the theme of the feast**
   Whether it is in a separate nook in your home, on a special shelf, or the center of your kitchen table, this space will help your children focus on the feast you celebrate. For example, collect and display holy cards or pictures illustrating different aspects of Our Lady. Candles and flowers whether real or artificial are a nice touch. Perhaps a lovely seashell or a handmade rosary would make your space especially Marian. Let each feast day spark your imagination. Encourage your children to make their own contributions.

2. **Prepare a Teatime Recipe**
   Within each feast you will find a suggested recipe for your teatime. These are simple to prepare. Some of the suggested recipes are feast specific or symbolic of the Marian celebration, but many are interchangeable and can be served on any of the feasts. Choose some and repeat them as you discover your favorites throughout the year if you wish. Just be sure to gather the ingredients you will need in advance. Also, you do not have to limit yourself to tea. There are certainly fruit juices, milk or water that could be used for any of these feast days. I encourage you to be creative whenever connections become clear. Please also be assured that any of your own family favorites may be more meaningful for a particular feast, so please feel free to select what you prefer, especially if your family has specific dietary needs.

3. **Choose a Devotional Activity**
   I offer a variety of hands-on activities for you to consider. You need not create a craft for each feast but I can vouch for the fact that doing so will greatly increase the level of fun, devotion to Mary, and creativity when celebrating. Plus, who doesn't like to make special things?
   For each craft activity, I provide directions and a list of materials. Again, I recommend gathering everything in advance so you can avoid scrambling at the last moment.

4. **Learn More**

   To enhance your celebration with a picture book or read-aloud book, or DVD viewing suggestion, please review the selections offered in Appendix A.

As a final thought, you may wish to create some sort of keepsake as a record of your *Mondays with Mary*. Taking photographs of your celebrations and then saving them in a Marian Notebook or Scrapbook might greatly enhance your memories and time together. This is certainly not required, but some just may find this immensely enjoyable! Scrapbooks and notebooks can be easily obtained at the craft store or online, you can even make your own, so please see the resources listed in Appendix C.

With these elements in place, you will be ready to begin *Mondays with Mary*. Please feel free to adapt this format to best suit your family or group situation. It is my hope and prayer that all who gather with you come to know Mary in a loving and special way.

For where two or three are gathered together in my name, there am I in the midst of them. —Matthew 18:20

Part 1

Mary, Our Mother

MARY
MOTHER OF GOD

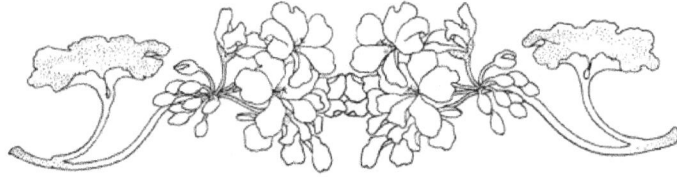

Holy Mary, pray for us.

Holy Name of Mary
September 12

"O name of Mary! Joy in the heart, honey in the mouth, melody to the ear of her devout clients!" —St. Anthony of Padua

The Holy Name of Mary is the first title of Mary in the *Litany of Loreto.* Today's celebration is all about revering Our Lady's name. "Mary" in Latin is *Maria*, in Hebrew it is *Maryam*, and in Aramaic it is *Miryam*. From this, the name "Mary" has been derived and it is so precious to us who call on her. Eight days after the birth of the Blessed Virgin Mary, in accordance with Jewish law, her parents, Saints Joachim and Anne, were inspired by their visions of angels to name her thus.

We do not really know much about Mary's parents, just how they yearned deeply for a child and implored God with fervent prayers, prayers God answered with the sweetest most delightful gift they—and we—could ever receive. It's important to note, too, that Saints Anne and Joachim are the grandparents of Our Lord. This is big!

"On this day dedicated to the Holy Name of Mary let us repeat that wonderful prayer of Saint Bernard: "Look to the star of the sea, call upon Mary ... in danger, in distress, in doubt, think of Mary, call upon Mary. May her name never be far from your lips, or far from your heart ... If you follow her, you will not stray; if you pray to her, you will not despair; if you turn your thoughts to her, you will not err. If she holds you, you will not fall; if she protects you, you need not fear; if she is your guide, you will not tire; if she is gracious to you, you will surely reach your destination." —Pope Benedict XVI (Address at Heiligenkreuz Abbey, September 9, 2007)

Teatime Chat

Do you know how you got your name? Did you know that God not only knew your name before you were born (Jeremiah 1:5) but knew how many hairs you would have on your head? (Luke 12:7) Have fun chatting today about how family members received their names. What does each name mean? Why is it special?

You might encourage the children to select or create a symbol for their names that they can use to decorate their notebooks or Marian scrapbooks as children of Mary and Jesus.

Thanking God for this feast of the *Holy Name of Mary* and for your family's special name days, ceremoniously mark each person's name day on the family calendar and chat about how these special days might be celebrated.

Devotional Activities (choose one or more)

♥ *Letters of Her Holy Name*

Supplies: 3- to 5- inch wood letters of your choice (one set or letter for each participant), acrylic craft paint in blue and white star, heart and flower stickers, Modge Podge™ or clear acrylic spray (optional).

Directions: Paint the large wooden letters blue or white to spell out M-A-R-Y, M-A-R-I-A, or A-V-E M-A-R-I-A and let dry. Decorate with the flower, star and heart stickers, seal with Modge Podge™ or clear acrylic spray if desired. Display on your Marian altar or at the dinner table.

♥ *Cross-Stitch or Embroider Marian Symbols*

Supplies: Assorted embroidery or cross stitch needles, assorted embroidery threads in blue, white, yellow or gold, fabric in white or blue, embroidery hoop, scissors.

Directions: Choose a Marian symbol to embroider or cross stitch and create a beautiful image for Our Lady. Try this simple "fleur de lis!"

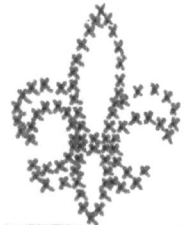

♥ Pray: *Litany of the Holy Name of Mary* (For private devotion only)

Lord, have mercy.
Lord, have mercy.
Christ, have mercy.
Lord, have mercy.
Son of Mary, hear us.
Son of Mary, graciously hear us.
Heavenly Father, of whom Mary
  is the Daughter, have mercy on us.
Eternal Word, of Whom Mary is the
Mother, Have Mercy on us
  Holy Spirit, of Whom Mary is the spouse,
      Have mercy on us
    Divine Trinity, of Whom Mary is the
      Handmaid, have mercy on us
Mary, Mother of the Living God, pray for us
  Mary, daughter of the Light Eternal,
      Mary, our light,
       Mary, our sister,
      Mary, flower of Jesse,
      Mary, issue of kings,
     Mary, chief work of God
    Mary, the beloved of God
   Mary, Immaculate Virgin
     Mary, all fair
    Mary, light in darkness
   Mary, our sure rest
    Mary, house of God
   Mary, sanctuary of the Lord
  Mary, altar of the Divinity
   Mary, Virgin Mother
Mary, embracing your Infant God
Mary, reposing with Eternal Wisdom
  Mary, ocean of bitterness.
    Mary, Star of the Sea
Mary, suffering with your only Son
Mary, pierced with a sword of sorrow
  Mary, torn with a cruel wound
  Mary, sorrowful even unto death
  Mary, bereft of all consolation
Mary, submissive to the law of God
Mary, standing by the Cross of Jesus
    Mary, Our Lady
    Mary, Our Queen
   Mary, Queen of glory
Mary glory of the Church Triumphant

Mary, Blessed Queen
Mary, advocate of the Church Militant
Mary, Queen of Mercy
Mary, consoler of the Church Suffering
Mary, exalted above the angels
Mary, crowned with twelve stars
Mary, fair as the moon
Mary, bright as the sun
Mary, distinguished above all
Mary, seated at the right hand of Jesus
Mary, our hope
Mary, our sweetness
Mary, glory of Jerusalem
Mary, joy of Israel
Mary, honor of our people
Mary, Our Lady of the Immaculate
    Conception
Mary, Our Lady of the Assumption
Mary, Our Lady of Loreto
Mary, Our Lady of Lourdes
Mary, Our Lady of Fatima
Mary, Our Lady of Czestochowa
Mary, Our Lady of the Miraculous Medal
Mary, Our Lady of Mount Carmel
Mary, Our Lady of the Angels
Mary, Our Lady of Dolors
Mary, Our Lady of Mercy
Mary, Our Lady of the Rosary
Mary, Our Lady of Victory
Mary, Our Lady of La Trappe
Mary, Our Lady of Divine Providence

Lamb of God, Who takes away the sins of the world, spare us, O Lord Jesus. Lamb of God, Who takes away the sins of the world, graciously hear us, O Lord Jesus. Lamb of God, Who takes away the sins of the world, have mercy on us, O Lord Jesus. Son of Mary, hear us. Son of Mary, graciously hear us.
I will declare your name unto my brethren.
I will praise you in the assembly of the faithful.

♥ **Sing:** *Ave Maris Stella* (see Appendix D)

Teatime Recipe Idea

Gingerbread Tea Cake

1 ½ c	unbleached all purpose flour	2 t	ground ginger
¼ c	sugar	¼ c	melted butter, cooled
1 t	baking powder	1 egg	beaten slightly
¼ t	baking soda	½ c	buttermilk
¼ t	salt	½ c	molasses
1 t	cinnamon		confectioners' sugar and whipped cream for garnish (optional)
¼ t	each grated nutmeg & ground cloves		

Directions: Butter and flour an 8″ or 9″ spring form pan with removable bottom or an 8″ square baking pan. Preheat oven to 350°F. In a large mixing bowl combine flour, sugar, salt, baking powder, soda and spices. Add the milk, melted butter, egg, and molasses and beat with an electric mixer on low speed or by hand until well combined. Pour the batter into your greased and floured pan. Bake for 25-35 minutes or until a toothpick inserted into the center of the cake comes out clean. Let the cake cool for 15 minutes in the pan, and then remove and let cool completely on a wire cooling rack. When the cake is completely cool, dust with powdered sugar and serve with a dollop of whip cream if you wish.

Holy Mary, pray for us!

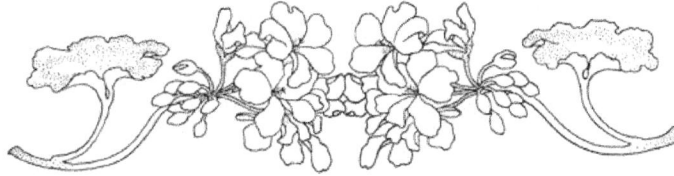

Holy Mother of God, pray for us.

Mary, the Mother of God
January 1

"A light will shine on us this day, the Lord is born for us: he shall be called Wonderful God, Prince of peace, Father of the world to come; and his kingship will never end."
—*Entrance antiphon, Solemnity of Mary, Mother of God*

The Solemnity of Mary, Mother of God begins the New Year on January 1. Celebrated during the twelve days of Christmas, it is a welcome feast day that acknowledges Mary's "yes" to God and her willingness to be the Mother of His son. In the *Litany of Loreto*, this second title sets the tone for the year ahead.

Just as she wrapped her new son in swaddling, Mary wraps us in her mantle of security, refuge, and grace. Whenever we seek her in prayer, she takes these prayers right to Our Lord, Jesus Christ. This special mantle of her motherhood is our protection and comfort. She is the Mother of the Christ, Our heavenly Mother, and Holy Mother of the Church all wrapped into one.

This feast is a good time to help children differentiate between how we venerate Mary as Mother of God and how we worship Jesus as Christ. Take this opportunity to explain that as the mediator of our petitions to Jesus, Mary can help us grow closer to her Son. Mary is our ultimate helper.

Start with prayer, and the best way to capture the attention of your audience is to have a bell or chime that serves as a call to pray. Monastics have used this technique for thousands of years, so why not you? My children always get excited when they hear the bell.

Begin by asking Jesus and Our Lady to bless your special time together, thanking them for this feast in Mary's honor.

Most children know how to pray the *Hail Mary*, so this would be a good way to start. Say three in honor of the Holy Trinity!

Teatime Chat

Since this feast falls so closely after the birth of Christ, the nativity story will still be fresh in your children's minds. You will want to read it again. Trust me, no child of mine ever tires of hearing it! Then, pose some questions based on these verses from Luke's Gospel:

> *And it came to pass, that when they were there, her days were accomplished, that she should be delivered. And she brought forth her firstborn son, and wrapped him up in swaddling clothes, and laid him in a manger; because there was no room for them in the inn. And there were in the same country shepherds watching, and keeping the night watches over their flock. And behold an angel of the Lord stood by them, and the brightness of God shone round about them; and they feared with a great fear. And the angel said to them: Fear not; for, behold, I bring you good tidings of great joy, that shall be to all the people: For, this day, is born to you a Saviour, who is Christ the Lord, in the city of David. And this shall be a sign unto you. You shall find the infant wrapped in swaddling clothes, and laid in a manger. And suddenly there was with the angel a multitude of the heavenly army, praising God, and saying: Glory to God in the highest; and on earth peace to men of good will. And it came to pass, after the angels departed from them into heaven, the shepherds said one to another: Let us go over to Bethlehem, and let us see this word that is come to pass, which the Lord hath showed to us. And they came with haste; and they found Mary and Joseph, and the infant lying in the manger. And seeing, they understood of the word that had been spoken to them concerning this child. And all that heard, wondered; and at those things that were told them by the shepherds. But Mary kept all these words, pondering them in her heart. And the shepherds returned, glorifying and praising God, for all the things they had heard and seen, as it was told unto them.* —Luke 2:6-20

How did Mary respond when the shepherds came and saw baby Jesus? What did the shepherds do after they returned to their fields? Presumably your nativity scene is still out and this would be a good time for the youngest children to play and arrange the pieces while the others are engaged in the discussion, but remember to ask what they think too!

Devotional Activities

♥ *Mary Candle*

Supplies: A 3-, 6- or 9-inch white pillar candle, water-based paint (wood craft paint works) silver and gold cross stickers, picture or holy card of Mary and baby Jesus, optional handkerchief or scrap of cloth cut into a square large enough to cover your candle, craft glue or glue stick.

Directions: Paint the pillar candle with the Chi-Rho ☧ symbol and let dry. Then glue a picture of Mary with the baby Jesus on to one side of the candle towards the bottom. Next decorate with the silver and gold cross stickers or you could also add other Marian symbols with paint or an indelible marker. This candle can be covered when not in use with any square of fabric, such as a handkerchief or a hemmed scrap of blue or white fabric. This creates the imagery of being covered in Mary's mantle of protection. Place your candle on a pretty plate or doily as a centerpiece for your celebration. Remember to let the wick cool before replacing the cloth.

♥ Sing: *On This Day, O Beautiful Mother*

♥ Recite: *Litany of Loreto*

9

♥ **Pray:** *"God, our Father, may we always profit by the prayers of the Virgin Mother Mary, for you bring us life and salvation through Jesus Christ her Son who lives and reigns with you and the Holy Spirit, one God, for ever and ever. Amen."* —Collect for this Feast

Teatime Recipe Idea

Nutella® Ladyfingers

Package of Ladyfingers (check your market)
Nutella® or melted chocolate chip morsels
Flaked coconut, preferably unsweetened

Milk
Vanilla extract
honey

Directions: Dip the Ladyfingers into Nutella® or melted chocolate chips, and then roll them in the coconut.

Make the Vanilla Milk Tea by heating the milk just to scalding and adding a ¼ teaspoon of vanilla extract and 1 Tablespoon honey, stir to combine and serve in pretty mugs or teacups.

Holy Mother of God, pray for us!

Holy Virgin of Virgins, pray for us.

Betrothal of Mary and Joseph
January 23

"Joseph, Son of David, have no fear about taking Mary as your wife. It is by the Holy Spirit that she has conceived this child. She is to have a son and you are to name him Jesus because he will save his people from their sins." —Matthew 1:20-22

Saint Joseph is the husband of Mary, the mother of Jesus. There is very little recorded in scripture about Joseph's life except for narratives in the gospels of Matthew and Luke. We know that Joseph was descended from David and that he and Mary lived in Nazareth after being married.

A betrothal is a true promise to marry, and, after having a vision from the archangel Gabriel about Mary having conceived Jesus by the Holy Spirit, Joseph took Mary as his wife. Joseph cared for Mary and Jesus from the beginning, worked as a carpenter and taught Jesus his trade. We suppose he passed away before Jesus began his public life.

We celebrate this feast of Mary's betrothal to Saint Joseph honoring her as the Holy Virgin of Virgins and it makes sense to talk about the birth of Our Lord again since we have recently celebrated the feast of Mary, the Mother of God.

Teatime Chat

Jesus was conceived in Mary through the Holy Spirit, therefore Joseph is the adoptive or foster father of Jesus. (On a practical level, you will need to explain this very carefully depending on the ages of your children). If you have adopted children, this is a wonderful opportunity to chat about the special blessing of adopting and being adopted. Again, the Nativity story in the gospel of either Matthew or Luke is perfect for your day!

Devotional Activities

♥ *Joseph and Mary's rings*

Supplies: cereal box or stiff cardstock in a neutral color, gold glitter paint, clear packing tape.

Directions: First, cut two cardboard or cardstock pieces into circles (one pair for each child) about 5 inches across, cutting out the center to create a ring (just like a donut). Next, cut a slit through the edge of one ring to the center opening. Now slide one ring into the center of the other ring. They will now be interlocking rings (think paper chain style). Then close up the slit with clear packing tape. Paint or decorate as desired to represent the wedding union of Joseph and Mary. Try gold glitter paint! An equally fun and perhaps less labor intensive idea that would work for very small children would be to make these like a paper chain with two pre-decorated paper or cardstock rings linked together.

♥ Pray: *Prayer to St. Joseph*

> *"O God, who has predestined St, Joseph from all eternity for the service of Thine Eternal Son and by His Blessed Mother, and made him worthy to be the spouse of the Blessed Virgin and the foster-father of Thy Son; we beseech Thee, through all the services He has rendered to Jesus and Mary on earth, that Thou would make us worthy of His intercession and grant us to enjoy the happiness of His company in heaven. Through Christ, Our Lord, Amen."* —Concluding prayer of St. Joseph Chaplet

Teatime Recipe Idea

Wedding Cupcakes

Bake white cupcakes and let the children have fun creating their own "wedding cakes" for Mary and Joseph. We like a white cream cheese icing sprinkled with coconut!

Cream Cheese Icing

1	pound cream cheese, softened	1-2 pounds confectioners' sugar, depending on how thick you like your icing!
2	sticks butter, softened	
½ t	coconut extract	
1 t	pure vanilla	

Directions: In the bowl of an electric mixer, blend together the cream cheese, butter and extracts. Gradually add enough confectioners' sugar to desired consistency and smooth. Frost cooled cupcakes and sprinkle generously with shredded unsweetened coconut.

Holy Virgin of Virgins, pray for us!

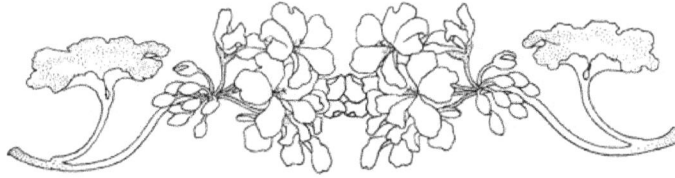

Mother of Christ, Mother of Our Creator, Mother of Our Savior, pray for us.

The Nativity of Jesus
December 25

Behold a virgin shall be with child, and bring forth a son, and they shall call his name Emmanuel, which being interpreted as, God with us.
—*Matthew 1:23*

We celebrate Mary, the virgin Mother of God today as *Mother of Christ, Mother of Our Creator,* and *Mother of Our Savior*. These titles in the *Litany of Loreto* are all-encompassing, honoring Mary's triumph over the disobedience of Eve. She is the Mother of our King and we rejoice with all the choirs of angels today. *"Glory to God in the highest; and on earth peace to men of good will."* (Luke 2:14)

With the nativity of Jesus as declared by the angels, our Savior has come and as his Mother, Mary helps to secure our happiness with God for all eternity. As *Mother of Our Creator*, Mary gave human nature to the Son of God, thus fulfilling the prophecy spoken in John: *"In the beginning was the Word, and the Word was with God, and the Word was God. The same was in the beginning with God. All things were made by Him: and without Him was made nothing that was made. In Him was life, and the life was the light of men."* (John 1:1-4)

Jesus came into the world to free the people from sin and as a result of Mary's obedience and absence of sin, she plays a part in our redemption as children of God. We have been greatly rewarded by Mary's dignity and her unfailing confidence in God. And because it is Christmas, we get to celebrate for twelve whole days!

Teatime Chat

Special note: You may choose to do this *Monday with Mary* at the beginning of Advent or sometime during Advent.

As we look to the nativity of Jesus and all the celebrations that accompany the Christmas season, let us remember how Mary said "yes" so willingly to God for all humankind.

What are some of your family's Christmas traditions? Why does it make celebrating and anticipating the birth of Jesus special for your family? How do your friends or other people you know celebrate Christmas? Do you know anyone who does not celebrate Jesus' birth?

Think about all these questions and discuss them together; you might even make a list of your favorites, and then give thanks to Mary for your Christmas traditions by honoring the birth of her Son, Jesus Christ, Our Savior and King in grand style.

Devotional Activities

♥ *Tea Box Nativity Scenes*

Supplies: Paper tea boxes sold in supermarkets such as *Twinnings*™ (one box per child), glue stick or craft glue, felt in assorted colors like brown, green and blue, 3 each small wood beads for heads, ½ walnut each shell for manger, moss or cotton wool for hay or snow, twigs, tiny pine branches, small pinecones, tiny faux bird nests, small plastic animals, pipe cleaners, fabric scraps or more felt.

Directions: If your tea box has already had the tea dispense opening removed then leave as is. If not, you will need to create an opening in the box on the lower half of one side. You can easily open the box and simply cut out part of one long side to create this opening. Next spread glue stick onto the inside of the box while it is opened and apply felt to cover the "walls" of the interior. Let dry and close up your box. Repeat by covering the exterior of the box with felt or a fabric color of your choice. There is even sticky-back felt sold in sheets at most craft stores. Now you can decorate as desired to create a small nativity scene. Create your Mary, Joseph and baby Jesus by drawing eyes, nose and mouth onto the wood beads. Next wrap some fabric or felt into a cloak shape for Mary and Joseph and a swaddling for baby Jesus. Glue the wood bead head onto your cloak and swaddling and place on the edge of your nativity box. Baby Jesus goes into the walnut shell half lined with some of the wool or felt hay. Display during Advent or for the Twelve days of Christmas!

Note: This can also be done with the café tins (such as *General Foods International Café Vienna* ™). Again decorate as desired and you have a small but delightful place for your smallest manger scenes.

♥ **Sing *Christmas Carols*** or go caroling around your neighborhood

♥ **Pray:**

> *"And there shall come forth a rod out of the root of Jesse, and a flower shall rise up out of his root. And the spirit of the Lord shall rest upon him: the spirit of wisdom, and of understanding, the spirit of counsel, and of fortitude, the spirit of knowledge, and of godliness. And he shall be filled with the spirit of the fear of the Lord."* —Isaiah 11:1-3

Teatime Recipe Idea

Bûche de Noël

*Special Note: This is a rather involved teatime treat, albeit lovely and traditional for Christmas; it may be more than you want to tackle. Feel free to substitute your own traditional holiday fare here, or even purchase a lovely *Bûche* at your local bakery. I've even been known to pull out a box of Twinkies and coat them with chocolate sauce.

¾ c	cake flour		¾ c	sugar
¾ t	baking powder		¼ t	salt
¼ t	salt		1 t	vanilla extract
5	eggs, separated into 2 bowls			

Directions: Preheat oven to 400°F and prepare a 10 ½ × 15 ½ × 1-inch jelly roll pan by greasing it, lining it with waxed or parchment paper, and then greasing it as well. Also have ready a larger sheet pan and a clean linen dish towel.

Sift together the flour, baking powder and salt, set aside. Beat the egg yolks until thick and pale. Gradually add six tablespoons of the sugar, beating well after each addition; the mixture should fall into a thick ribbon when the beaters are lifted. Add the vanilla and beat again.

With clean dry beaters, beat the egg whites until foamy. Gradually add the remaining sugar, beating constantly, until the whites stand in firm, glossy, moist peaks. Fold a third of the whites into the yolk mixture to lighten it; fold the rest of the egg whites into the lightened yolk mixture.

Using a fine strainer, gradually sift the dry ingredients into the egg mixture, folding them in gently but thoroughly. Spread the batter evenly in the prepared pan, making sure to get it into the corners. Put the pan in the oven immediately.

Bake for 10-12 minutes, or just until the cake is golden on top and tester inserted in the center comes out clean. Do not over bake.

Working quickly, cover the pan first with the dishtowel and then with the cookie sheet. Turn over the cookie sheet, towel and pan to turn out the cake. Remove the smaller cookie sheet that you baked on and then peel off the parchment paper. Slide the towel and cake onto the counter or table; the cake is wrong side up. Cut off any crisp edges, fold one end of the towel over the short end of the cake and roll up the cake in the towel. Place the cake seam-side down onto a wire rack to cool completely. (See frosting recipes below before proceeding with the rest).

Unroll the cooled cake leaving it on the towel and spread ½ cup of the Mocha Silk Frosting evenly over the cake, all the way to the edges. Spread 2 cups of the Buttercream Frosting over the thin layer of mocha pushing a generous amount into the curved end. Roll up again without the towel but using the towel to help guide your roll. Place cake seam side down on a cake plate or tray. Use a small spatula to remove any excess filling from the ends and seam edge. Refrigerate for about an hour to firm the filling.

Trim and taste ☺ a thin slice from the end of the chilled cake; cut and reserve a wedge from the other end. Spread a little leftover butter cream on the top of the cake and press the reserved wedge into it to make a "knothole."

Now frost the entire cake with the remaining mocha silk frosting building the frosting up around the sides of the knothole leaving the top free of frosting. Repeatedly draw a narrow spatula lengthwise through the frosting to simulate the rough texture of the bark. Decorate as desired to make your bûche de noël, as "log-like" as desired.

Buttercream Frosting

½ c	superfine sugar	7-8 T	heavy cream
1	egg yolk	½ c + 2T	butter, softened
pinch	salt	2 ⅓ c	sifted confectioners'
1 ½ t	vanilla extract		sugar

Directions: Combine the sugar, egg yolk, salt, vanilla and 2 ½ tablespoons of the cream and beat for eight minutes at medium speed in the bowl of an electric mixer. In a large bowl, cream ½ cup of the butter until light. Add the yolk mixture a little at a time, beating well after each addition. Gradually add two cups of the confectioners' sugar, beating well after each addition. Makes 2 ½ to 3 cups frosting.

Mocha Silk Frosting

1¾ c   confectioners' sugar
3 T   unsweetened cocoa powder
2 t   powdered instant coffee
5 ⅓ T butter, softened

1 ½ T light corn syrup
1 t   vanilla extract
2-4 T   heavy cream

Directions: Sift together and then stir the sugar, cocoa and coffee. Add the butter, corn syrup, vanilla and two tablespoons cream and beat for a minute at medium speed. Add just enough of the remaining cream to make the frosting easy to spread.

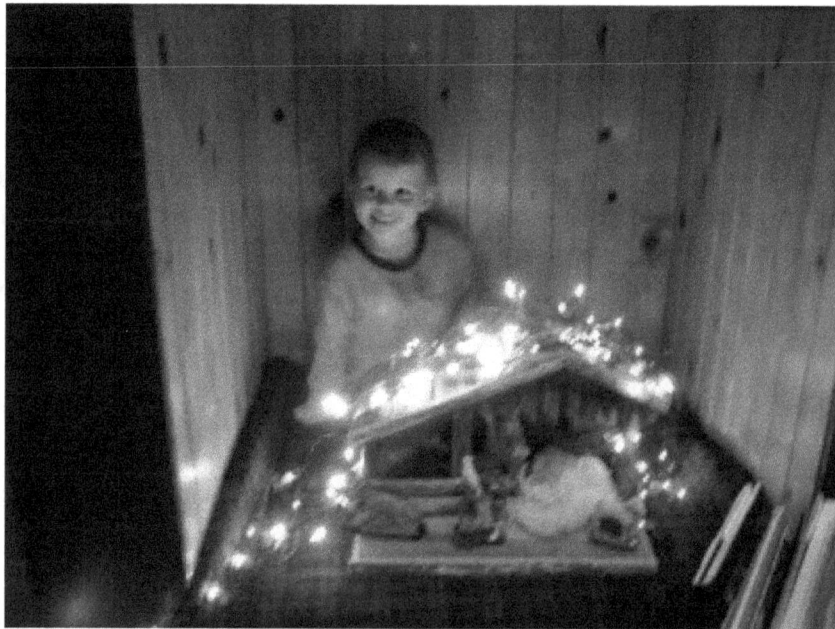

Mother of Christ, Mother of Our Creator, Mother of Our Savior, pray for us!

Mother of Divine Grace, pray for us.

Our Lady, Virgin of Grace
June 9

"We fly to your patronage, O holy Mother of God, despise not our petitions in our necessities, but deliver us always from all dangers, O glorious and blessed Virgin." —(Sub Tuum)

Our Lady is known as Mother of Divine Grace in the *Litany of Loreto* just after her title of Mother of Christ. She is celebrated as Our Lady, Virgin of Grace today as God bestowed upon Mary all His heavenly graces in order to be the Mother of His son. Mary also increased in grace throughout Her life, and yearns to bestow the true grace of God upon us. Mary's grace comes from God – she is "full of grace" and she wishes to help us grow in love of God so that we too may obtain the grace we need to get to heaven. If only we can deepen our understanding of Her advocacy with Her Son, Her intercessory power, Her unending ability to seek out mercy for us. Mary is our advocate beyond compare.

> *"The grace of Christ is the gratuitous gift that God makes to us of His own life, infused by the Holy Spirit into our soul to heal it of sin and to sanctify it. It is the sanctifying or deifying grace received in Baptism. It is the source of the work of sanctification."* —Catechism of the Catholic Church, 1999

Teatime Chat

There is an English hymn from the fourteen century that recalls Mary as a "rose without a thorn" and having *gratia divina* or divine grace. Have you ever found a rose without a thorn?

Because Mary had been given sanctifying grace in Her Immaculate Conception, she is the true source to whom we can go for spiritual healing and to receive the gifts of grace from Jesus. God is the author of grace and He chose Mary to be one of the pages on which He wrote salvation history.

What Bible stories can you recall where God showered His gifts of grace on His chosen people? How about Jonah and the Whale, or Daniel and the Lion's Den? What about the story of Abraham and Sarah, or when God rained down manna from heaven so the Israelites wouldn't starve?

How about a time where God showed His good graces for your family, perhaps with the birth of a new brother or sister, or a new job for a parent, or a new home? God imparts His graces upon His people in many different ways.

Devotional Activities

♥ **Create:** *Wreath of Good Graces*

Supplies: Cardboard cereal box or pre-made twig or faux greenery wreath, flower stickers or artificial flowers.

Directions: Using either a piece of cardboard cut into the shape of a wreath and painted green or a pre-made twig or greenery wreath from the craft store, begin by adding flower stickers or silk flowers each time a special deed is performed in Mary's honor, such as saying a "hail Mary" or reciting the "Memorare" prayer. This could be a special summertime devotion to end on the Assumption if desired!

♥ **Pray:** *"O God, You gave the human rave the grace of forgiveness through the virginal motherhood of the Blessed Virgin Mary; grant that we who call her the Mother of Grace on earth, may enjoy her happy presence forever in heaven. We ask this through the same Christ Our Lord."* Amen. —Feast of the Virgin Mother of Grace (prayer from *Our Lady's Titles*, Fr. Lawrence G. Lovasik, S.V.D.)

Teatime Recipe Idea

Baked Apples with Raisins and Nuts *(These will be even more tempting than the "one" Adam and Eve ate)*

6-8 Large Tart Apples such as Macintosh
    (or enough for each person to have ½ an apple)
Chopped Walnuts or Pecans,
Raisins
Whipped Cream (optional)

⅔ c   brown sugar, packed
½ t   ground ginger
1 t   cinnamon

Directions: Preheat oven to 350°F. Core the apples to within ½ inch of the bottom of the apple, but not through. Combine all the ingredients except the whipped cream and fill each apple cavity packing in gently to the top. Dot each top with butter and place into a baking pan and fill with hot water. Cover and bake about 45 minutes or until the apples and tender, but not applesauce ☺. Let cool slightly, then slice each apple in half and discard bottom core parts. Serve warm with a dollop of whip cream and a dusting of cinnamon.

Mother of Divine Grace, pray for us!

Forget-me-nots, Mary's Eyes

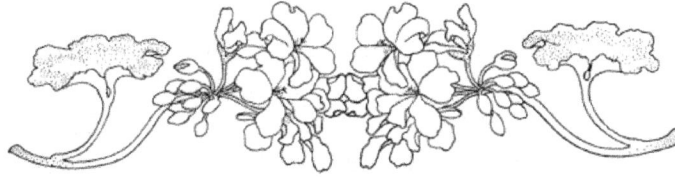

Mother Most Pure, Mother Most Chaste, Mother Most Inviolate, Mother Most Undefiled, pray for us.

The Purification of Our Lady (Presentation of Our Lord)
February 2

"The Snowdrop, in purest white arraie
First rears her head on Candlemas daie . . ."

The Presentation of Jesus in the Temple is also the Feast of the Purification of Mary. Mary in her title as Mother Undefiled was completely free from sin and pure before, during and after the birth of Christ. The motherhood and virginity of Mary remain a mystery for all Christianity; not to be solved, but to contemplate. As we celebrate this ninth title of Mary in the *Litany of Loreto*, we will include her titles Mother Most Pure, Mother Most Chaste, and Mother Inviolate since they all represent Her purity and goodness.

Much can be discovered by studying the scripture passages relative to this feast. Mary followed Hebrew purification laws written in Leviticus, "The priest shall make atonement for her sin, and thus she will be made clean." (Leviticus 12:8). Jewish women were required to offer a ritual sacrifice and receive a blessing in the Temple forty days after giving birth. Being completely pure and undefiled, Mary did not have to undergo this ritual, but did so anyway as an obedient woman of God.

> *"When the day came to purify them according to the law of Moses, the couple brought him up to Jerusalem so that he could be presented to the Lord, for it is written in the law of the Lord, 'Every first-born male shall be consecrated to the Lord.' They came to offer in sacrifice 'a pair of turtledoves or two young pigeons,' in accord with the dictate of the law of the Lord."*
> —Luke 2:22-24

When Jesus was presented at the Temple, Simeon proclaimed the infant would be, "A revealing light to the Gentiles, the glory of your people Israel." (Luke 2:32) As a result, we also refer to this feast as *Candlemas.* Some parishes offer a special Mass and bless candles on this day to remind us that Jesus is the "Light of the world." Today's feast is exactly forty days from Christmas.

Teatime Chat

We focus on Mary's purity and obedience to God as she and Saint Joseph take their newborn son to the Temple. Joseph and Mary marveled at all that was said about their young son, and they remained pious and serene and took him home to be raised as any new baby in Nazareth. Our feast today gives us some great symbolism to draw from for our discussion. As Mary and Joseph were poor they brought with them a pair of doves to the temple. And with the prophecy of Simeon, we have an affirmation that Jesus is indeed the light of the world as revealed to be a saving grace to the Israelites.

If you chose candles for a symbol, they are meant to represent Jesus' never ending light as redeemer of the world and therefore candles have been blessed and lit on this day for many centuries. The doves are a sign of purity and poverty or sacrifice. Do you know what other church feast has the great symbol of a dove?

Devotional Activities (choose one or more)

♥ **Create: *Origami White Doves in a Basket*** (Origami White Doves)

Supplies: Thin white paper (origami paper if you have it and you'll need at least two sheets for each child), small basket or plate for each child's finished doves.

Directions: Fold origami paper into a dove shape and place two in each basket or plate. *Note: I found a wonderful tutorial for folding origami doves at (http://www.origami-instructions.com/origami-dove.html) Happy folding!

♥ ***Decorated Votives*** (for blessed candles) to reflect the offering from Mary and Joseph and to symbolize Jesus as the "light to the Gentiles."

Supplies: Small clear glass votive holders (one per child) dove stickers, indelible marking pen in white (optional). Blessed tea lights.

Directions: Decorate the votives with the dove stickers or hand paint doves onto each votive. Insert a tea light into each votive light and display on a mantle for evening prayer.

♥ **Pray: *Final day of the Novena for Purification***

> *"O Blessed Mother of God, who went up to the Temple according to the law with your offering of little white doves, pray for me that I too may keep the law and be pure in heart like you. Sweet heart of Mary be my salvation."*

♥ **Pray: *Fourth Joyful Mystery***

♥ **Copywork: Canticle of Simeon**

> *"Lord, now let your servant go in peace, your word has been fulfilled. My own eyes have seen the salvation which you've prepared in the sight of every people. A light to reveal you to the nations and the glory of your people Israel. Glory Be to the Father, and to the Son, and to the Holy Spirit, as it was in the beginning, is now, and ever shall be, world without end." Amen. -* —(Luke 2:29-32)

Teatime Recipe Idea

A Candlelight Dinner would be appropriate for this feast.

Dove Shaped Cookies (use refrigerator sugar cookies for convenience if you like)

Mother Most Pure, Mother Most Chaste, Mother Most Inviolate, Mother Most Undefiled, pray for us!

Snowdrop for Candlemas

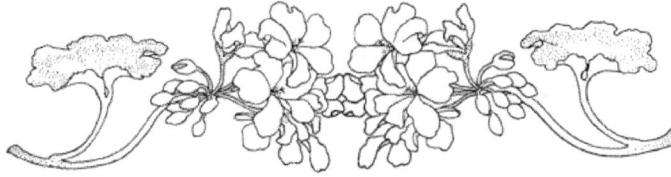

Mother Most Amiable, Mother Most Admirable,Pray for us.

The Immaculate Heart of Mary
Saturday following the 2nd Sunday after Pentecost

That is why I warn you, do not be concerned for your life, what you are to eat, or for your body, what you are to wear. Seek out instead his kingship over you, and the rest will follow in turn. Do not live in fear, little flock . . . Sell what you have and give alms. Get purses for yourselves that do not wear out, a never-failing treasure with the Lord which no thief comes near nor any moth destroys. Wherever your treasure lies, there your heart will be." —(Luke 12:22, 31-34)

In connection with the strong devotion of the faithful to the *Sacred Heart of Jesus*, a separate feast for Our Lady honoring her Immaculate Heart was instituted. We look to her in this title as *Mother Most Amiable* and *Mother Most Admirable*. The Blessed Mother is truly one to admire. She is a fountain of goodness and to be revered as a trustworthy advocate for us. Much like our celebration of Mary's Purification on February 2, today we devote ourselves to Mary's sweet heart and ask for her help in all we do.

Teatime Chat

Simeon's prophecy at *The Presentation of Jesus in the Temple* paved the way for this devotion with the imagery that Mary's heart would be pierced with a sword. In Luke's Gospel we read that Mary kept all the sayings and doings of Jesus in her heart throughout her lifetime, that she might ponder them and live by them. (Luke 2:33-34)

The scriptures tell us that we should store up our treasures and that is where our heart will be. (Matthew 6:20-21) Mary is our treasure here on earth. She wants us to come to her and gather up our treasures while we are living our everyday lives that we may one day be united with God, our ultimate treasure! When we say the rosary, pray for someone's intentions invoking the Mother of God, and begging for her assistance in asking for God's mercy towards us, this is storing up our treasure for heaven! How many treasures can you collect today? How about in a week, or a month?

Pictures of Mary's Immaculate Heart are shown with the sword piercing through the top and a ring of roses encircling the whole heart. This imagery helps us to think of the sorrow and suffering of Mary as well as her joy and beauty she gave the world through her Son. In 1942, Pope Pius XII consecrated the world to the Immaculate Heart of Mary. (Please see *Our Lady of Fatima, Queen of Peace* for more ideas on consecrating yourself and your family to the Immaculate Heart of Mary).

Devotional Activities

♥ *Immaculate Heart Treasure Boxes*

Supplies: Small unpainted wood boxes or small treasure-type chests, wood paints, stickers, small imitation flowers, foam hearts, glue stick or craft glue.

Directions: Decorate boxes with wood paint and let dry. Embellish dried boxes as you wish to make it beautiful for Our Lady. Immaculate Heart symbols would be lovely! After the boxes are complete, have the children write out a treasure on a slip of paper such as "Jesus, Mary Joseph, I love you" and place it in their box. Encourage them to add to it regularly with these simple and easy prayers. Here are few more ideas of treasures for Mary and Jesus:

> *Sweet Heart of Mary, be my salvation, O Mary, conceived without sin, pray for us who have recourse to Thee, Pray for us O Holy Mother of God, that we may be made worthy of the promises of Christ.*

See how many treasures they can "store up."

♥ Pray:

Father, You prepared the heart of the Virgin Mary to be a fitting home for Your Holy Spirit. By her prayers may we become a more worthy temple of Your glory. Grant this through our Lord Jesus Christ, Your Son, who lives and reigns with You and the Holy Spirit, one God, for ever and ever. —Collect for the Feast of the Immaculate Heart of Mary.

Teatime Recipe Idea

Immaculate Heart Window Cookies

Here is a basic "*Linzer*" cookie recipe:

3 sticks	unsalted butter, room temperature	3 ½ c	all purpose flour
1 c	sugar	¼ t	salt
1 t	vanilla extract	¾ c	raspberry preserves
			Confectioners' sugar for dusting

Directions: Preheat oven to 350°F. In the bowl of an electric mixer fitted with the paddle attachment, mix together the butter and sugar until they are just combined. Add the vanilla. In another bowl, sift together the flour and salt, then add them to the butter mixture on low speed. When the dough starts to come together dump out onto a surface dusted with flour and shape into flat disc. Wrap in plastic and chill for 20 to 30 minutes.

Roll the dough ¼ inch thick and cut with a 3″ – 4″ heart shaped cookie cutter. Cut an equal number of the hearts with a smaller cutter to make the "window" pieces. Place all the cookies onto a cookie sheet and chill again for another 15 minutes or so. Bake the cookies for 20 – 25 minutes until the edges begin to just brown. Allow to cool to room temperature. Spread the raspberry preserves on the whole cookies and top with a "window" gently pressing the cookie into the jam. Dust with confectioners sugar if desired. Serve on a plate surrounded by rose petals to represent Our Lady's Immaculate Heart!

Mother Most Amiable, Mother Most Admirable, pray for us!

Petunia, symbol of Our Lady's Praises

Part 2

Mary, Ever-Virgin

Our Lady of Good Counsel

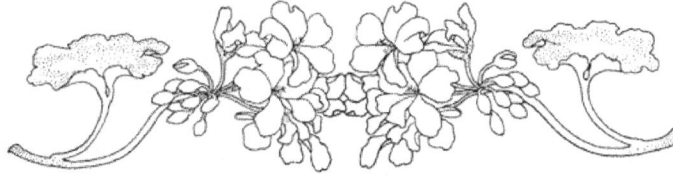

Mother of Good Counsel, Virgin Most Prudent, pray for us.

Mother of Good Counsel, Virgin Most Prudent
April 26

"O Mary of Good Counsel, inflame the hearts of all who are devoted to you, so that all of them have shelter in you, O great Mother of God. O most worthy Lady, let everyone choose you as teacher and wise counselor of their souls, since you are, as Saint Augustine says, the counsel of the Apostles and counsel of all peoples."

—Prayer to Implore Protection from Our
Lady of Good Counsel, c. 1796

Today we honor Mary in her Litany titles *Mother of Good Counsel* and *Virgin Most Prudent*. You can do this tea on April 26, the Feast of Our Lady of Good Counsel.

Mother of Good Counsel

In Genazzano, Italy, there is a church that enshrines the original image of *Our Lady of Good Counsel* which miraculously appeared there on the Feast of St. Mark in 1467. The townspeople were celebrating this feast when a cloud descended upon the unfinished and roofless church and suddenly the image of the Madonna and Child was revealed perching on a ledge where it remains today. This miraculous event has increased devotion to Our Lady under this title and was inserted into the *Litany of Loreto* in 1903 by Pope Leo XIII.

35

Virgin Most Prudent

We know that Mary practiced prudence all throughout her life. She was silent and wisely kept things to herself; in fact, there are only seven occasions on which her words were recorded. If we look at those few recorded instances, we see how wise and prudent her words were. Because of her prudence and wisdom, she became counselor and confidante to the Apostles and many other followers of Jesus after his death. Even as Jesus hung dying on the cross, she stood by silently as her heart was pierced. In that moment Jesus gives her as mother to the Apostle John and ultimately to us. The apostles most likely depended on Mary's nurturing spirit to guide them during the uncertain times after Jesus' death and after His Ascension. And we can depend on her prudent guidance as well

In Psalm 110:10 we read, "The fear of the Lord is the beginning of wisdom." Mary loved God above all things with her whole heart and set forth a perfect example by leading a life of humility and sacrifice. "Happy are they who fear the Lord, who walk in his ways! For you shall eat the fruit of your handiwork; happy shall you be, and favored" (Psalm 128:1-2). Our Lady wisely gave her entire and undivided love to God. As we honor Mary in these titles today, may we seek to have the good sense to walk in His ways.

Teatime Chat

What does it mean to give counsel to someone? What does it means to be prudent, or to do something with prudence? Our Lady not only gives us counsel with her intercession to Jesus for us, but she always uses prudence and delights us with the grace of God when we ask for it.

Discuss some different times when it might have been better to have practiced prudence (saving that piece of chocolate cake for after dinner). Has anyone ever asked for your advice or counsel? What advice did you give them and did you feel like they benefited from your wise words?

Our Lady is always there to give us counsel and help us to make prudent decisions. She will pour out the grace of God each time we ask!

Devotional Activities

♥ Read the story of how the painting appeared miraculously, where it came from, and what was going on in Genazzano at the time. It's a beautiful story. You can find the story in numerous places on the Internet. Here is a simple version: http://www.traditioninaction.org/religious/a004rp.htm. Make a storyboard of the events of the miraculous appearance. (A storyboard is a page or poster board with a series of pictures that tell a story.)

♥ Create your own holy card of the image of Our Lady of Good Counsel

Cut a piece of card stock or heavy paper and trace the image of Our Lady of Good Counsel on it (use the image on page 33). Color it. Print a prayer on the back: *Mother of Good Counsel, pray for us* and *Virgin Most Prudent, pray for us.*

♥ *Beatitudes Banner*

The Beatitudes are Christ's instructions to us on how to live, and Mary's life exemplifies them. Through devotion to Mary and by imitating her, we can live a more simple and prudent life.

Supplies: Large (8 ½ × 11 inches or larger) pieces of construction paper or poster board, markers, crayons or colored pencils, yarn or ribbon, hole punch, glue stick

Directions: Provide copies of the Beatitudes from Matthew 5:3-12 for your children to cut out and paste onto their paper or poster board. If they desire, they can write them out with beautiful script. Decorate banners further as desired, hole punch each top corner, and then insert a piece of yarn or ribbon long enough to create a hanger. Display and recite often!

♥ **Pray:** *The Beatitudes* and think of how Mary's life illustrates each of them.

> *"Blessed are the poor in spirit: for theirs is the kingdom of heaven. Blessed are the meek: for they shall possess the land. Blessed are they that mourn: for they shall be comforted. Blessed are they that hunger and thirst after justice: for they shall have their fill. Blessed are the merciful: for they shall obtain mercy. Blessed are the clean of heart: for they shall see God. Blessed are the peacemakers: for they shall be called children of God. Blessed are they that suffer persecution for justice' sake: for theirs is the*

*kingdom of heaven. Blessed are ye when they shall revile you,
and persecute you, and speak all that is evil against you, untruly,
for my sake: Be glad and rejoice, for your reward is very great in
heaven."* —Matthew 5:3-12

Teatime Recipe Idea

Perfect Scones— *Representing the Perfections of Mary*

(As perfected and offered by my dear daughter Emma Grace)

2 c	all purpose flour		6 T	butter, chilled & cut into
1 T	baking powder			chunks
2 T	sugar		¼ c	melted butter
½ t	salt			
½ c	buttermilk			Cinnamon sugar for topping

Directions: Mix together all the dry ingredients. Cut in the chilled butter chunks with your fingertips or a pastry blender. Mixture should resemble coarse cornmeal. Make a well in the dry ingredients and pour in buttermilk. Mix until just combined. Pour out dough onto a floured surface and gently press dough into a ½ inch round disc. Cut into 8 triangles (or other desired shape); brush the tops with the melted butter and sprinkle with cinnamon sugar. Bake at 425°F for 15 to 20 minutes or until lightly golden.

Mother of Good Counsel, Virgin Most Prudent, pray for us!

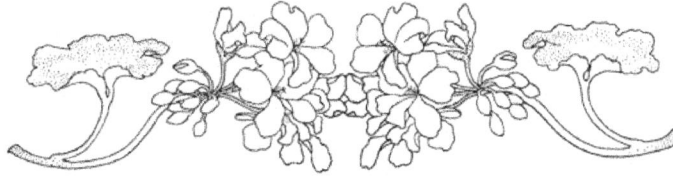

Virgin Most Venerable, pray for us.

The Presentation of the Blessed Virgin Mary
November 21

"The root of Jesse has produced a sweet stalk, from which has come a flower filled with a wondrous fragrance."
—Antiphon, The Magnificat, II Vespers,
Feasts of Sts. Anne and Joachim

We seek devotion to Mary today as Virgin Most Venerable and cherish this feast as a sign of Mary's life of purity and faith.

When Saints Joachim and Anne prayed for a child, it is not clear that they ever knew just how special their little child would be. What they did know, is that if they were ever granted such a gift from God, they would surely dedicate her to God in the temple. The legend that follows is their story and has been incorporated in to our Catholic traditions as a sure sign of God's love for His people and His goodness.

In his book, *Mary the Mother of Jesus* (Holiday House, 1995), Tomie dePaola describes the Presentation of Mary in the temple. Here is simple retelling of dePaola's story:

Saints Joachim and Anne were from the royal house of David. They were faithful to God, but sad because they had no children. "One evening ... Anne was walking in the garden. She saw a nest of baby birds and began to cry because she was childless."
An angel appeared to her and told her that she would have a child—a daughter—who would be a blessing to the world. An angel also appeared to Joachim, who was praying in the hills, and told him the same thing. They met at the city gates and rejoiced together.

When their baby was born, they named her Mary. And, when she was three years old, Joachim and Anne took her to be presented at the temple. The high priest blessed her saying, "Mary, the Lord has magnified your name to all generations. In you shall be made known the redemption of all Israel." Mary danced with joy and was loved by all.

Be sure to check out this book to read the entire story and many others about the life of Mary.

This feast also commemorates the dedication of the Church of St. Mary that was built in Jerusalem close to the site of the Temple.

Teatime Chat

Do you know anyone or does anyone in your family share St. Anne's name? St. Anne happens to be my patron namesake and so I have quite an affinity to her beautiful story and believe that each time we have a child in our family and offer them up to God through Baptism, it's a little bit of heaven here on earth and possibly a little bit like what Sts. Anne and Joachim must have experienced when they gave young Mary to the high priests at the temple.

Can you imagine giving your child over to the high priests at the temple at such a tender age? This was the custom at the time that Mary lived, and we suppose that young Mary *skipped and danced up the steps to the temple all by herself!* What a joyful heart she must have had! Mary's dedication to the Lord at such a young age is a true testimony of her fidelity and oneness with God in her Immaculate Conception, and we have Sts. Joachim and Anne to thank for her.

Devotional Activities

♥ *A Stitch in Time with St. Anne*, patron of needle workers

*Special Note: Any sewing, embroidery or simple stitching techniques could be used for today's activity. I would like to recommend a beautiful book by Alice Cantrell, *Sewing With St. Anne* (Little Way Press, 2005) available through Catholic Heritage Curricula (see Resource Appendix C). There are many very simple and lovely projects that could accompany today's feast, or be worked on over several days. The idea is to just get started stitching, it would be a lovely tribute to Our Lady and Good St. Anne.

Possible supplies: variety of needles including plastic yarn needles for the smallest workers, embroidery thread in several colors, yarn, embroidery hoops, white cotton material such as a flour sack, white handkerchief or Aida cloth (all available at most fabric stores) or maybe your own personal fabric stash.

Alternatively, children three and older can try these simple stitch patterns found at Primrose Design. Here is her online stitch guide in a downloadable format at (www.primrosedesign.com/emb_patterns.html) A sampler of all the stitches could be made by more experienced and enthusiastic children!

♥Pray: *Prayer to St. Anne*

Remember, O glorious and Good Saint Ann, that never was it known that anyone who fled to thy protection, implored thy help and sought thy intercession, was left unaided. Inspired by this confidence, behold, I cast myself at thy feet, and beseech thee, by thy great prerogative of being the Mother of the Queen of Heaven and the Grandmother of Jesus, come to my aid with thy powerful intercession, and obtain from Almighty God through the ever Blessed Virgin Mary, this special favor which I beg of thee . . .

Cease not to intercede for me until, through Divine Mercy, my request may be granted. Above all, obtain for me the grace one day to behold my God face to face and with thee and Mary and all the Saints praise and bless Him through all eternity. Amen.

Teatime Recipe Idea

St. Anne's Bird's Nests

Melt 12 oz. Chocolate morsels/chips over a simmering double boiler until smooth, stirring occasionally. Pour cooled chocolate over plain chow-mien noodles until completely covered. Spread spoonfuls of the chocolate noodles onto wax paper covered cookie sheet and use your fingers to form little nests. Fill with a few jellybeans for eggs and you have some sweet and adorable bird nests.

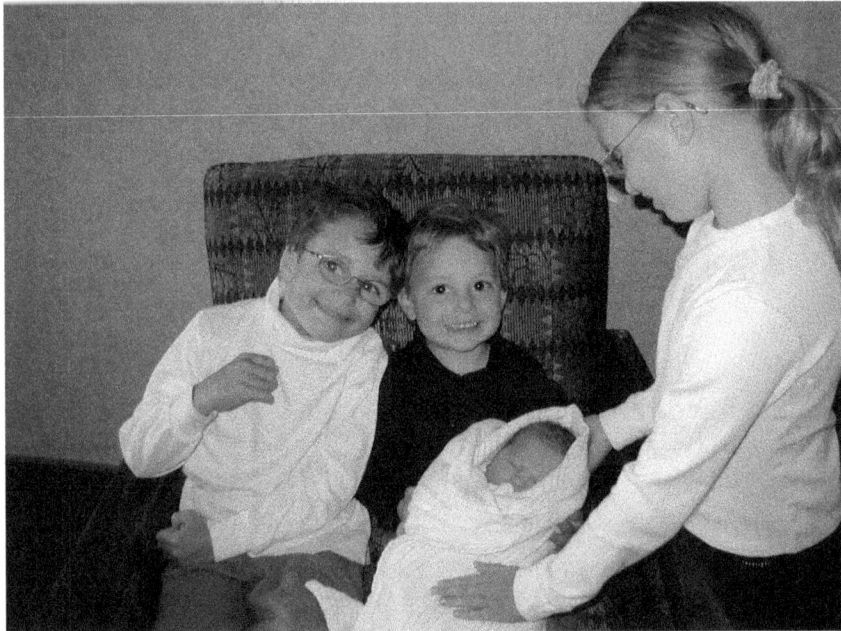

Virgin Most Venerable, pray for us!

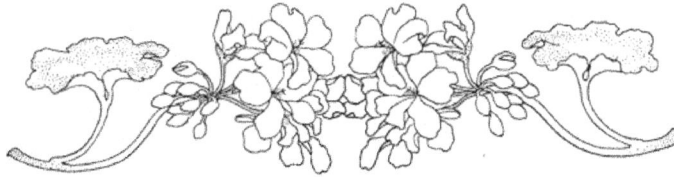

Virgin Most Renowned, pray for us.

Solemnity of the Annunciation of Our Lord
March 25

"As a lily among brambles, so is my love among maidens."
—Song of Songs 2:2

The Solemnity of the Annunciation of Our Lord is the first Joyful Mystery of the Rosary and celebrated nine months prior to the Birth of Our Lord. In England it is referred to as "Lady Day" and this is a day for honoring Christ within the womb of his mother.

Mary is the Virgin Most Renowned because she is the Mother of God. The angel Gabriel declared this with his announcement to her. Her yes to God would change the salvation history for all mankind forever. When Mary said, "Let is be done to me as you say," (Luke 1:38b) she humbly accepted the will of the Father. No other woman on earth holds the esteem of Our Lord's good graces like the woman that is Mary. Mary is the ever-virgin mother of God over-shadowed by the Holy Spirit. She is and always has been ready for God's overflowing love and grace.

"Mary said: I am the servant of the Lord" (Luke 1:38a). Even when Mary asks the angel, "How can this be . . .?" (Luke 1:34) she still had indefatigable trust in Our Lord and accepted the angel's words as God's Word. Period, no discussion! "The word became flesh . . ." (John 1:1).

Teatime Chat

Show your children the painting *The Angelus* by Jean-Francois Millet (1859). It is probably the most famous of his works, and is simply beautiful in

43

its representation of the faithful pausing for prayer during their work in the field. This beautiful devotion in honor of the Incarnation of Our Lord and veneration of His Blessed Mother as a form of commemorating the Annunciation is recited at morning, noon, and evening at the sound of a bell rung in many churches, religious houses, and institutions. From early times the ringing of the bells consisted of nine strokes in groups of three with a pause between. However, nowadays, this is followed by a series of nine even strokes. In so many countries the Angelus was, and is, particularly associated with peace arising from the tradition that the Annunciation took place in the peace of the evening.

You can share with your children about how waffles were traditionally served throughout Europe for just about any feast day, but that they were always thought best for Lady Day, or the *Solemnity of the Annunciation of Our Lord*

Mary garden lore tells of the flora attributed to this feast is the Madonna Lily or Annunciation Lily. It is said that as the angel Gabriel hailed Mary, he was holding a white lily. It is also said that as Mary was Assumed into Heaven by Jesus, that she was surrounded by roses and lilies.

Devotional Activities

♥ *Annunciation Bells*

Supplies: Find single bells at the craft store or use jingle bells sold readily during holiday time. You may also purchase miniature bells sold with most Mass Kits sold online or at Catholic Religious stores (see Resource Appendix D), ribbon or an assortment of yarns.

Directions: Tie the bells with ribbon or yarns. Different ribbons to represent the color of the liturgical seasons would be nice, green for Ordinary Time, purple for Advent and Lent, white for Christmas. After you tie them onto your bells, ring them every time you want to say your Angelus!

♥ *Art Appreciation* The Angelus by Millet (1859) *Special Note: you can easily find a copy of Millet's *Angelus* with a quick online search, or better yet, plan ahead and acquire an art appreciation book from the library before today's feast!

♥ **Pray:** *The Angelus*

> *V. The Angel of the Lord declared unto Mary.*
> *R. "And she conceived of the Holy Ghost."*
> *Hail Mary, Full of grace...*
> *V. Behold the handmaid of the Lord.*
> *R. "May it be done unto me according to Thy Word"*
> *Hail Mary, Full of grace...*
> *V. And the Word was made flesh.*
> *R. "And dwelt among us."*
> *Hail Mary, Full of grace...*
> *V. Pray for us O holy Mother of God*
> *R. "That we may be made worthy of the promises of Christ"*

> *All: Pour forth we beseech thee O Lord, thy grace into our hearts, that we to whom the Incarnation of Christ thy Son was made known by the message of an angel, may by His passion and cross be brought to the glory of his resurrection through the same Christ Our Lord. Amen.*

Teatime Recipe Idea

Annunciation Waffles

The waffles can be served at breakfast or as a special dessert.

1 ¾ c	heavy cream	¼ t	salt
1 ⅓ c	all purpose flour	½ c	cold water
2 T	sugar	3-4 T	melted sweet-cream butter

Directions: Whip the cream until stiff. Mix the flour, sugar, salt in a bowl. Stir in the water to make a smooth batter. Fold in the whipped cream, then stir in the melted butter.

Cook waffles according to your manufacturers waffle maker until crisp. Place on a rack to keep crisp while the others cook. Serve with fresh fruit, syrup and more whipped cream. Alternatively these would be lovely drizzled with melted chocolate!

Virgin Most Renowned, pray for us!

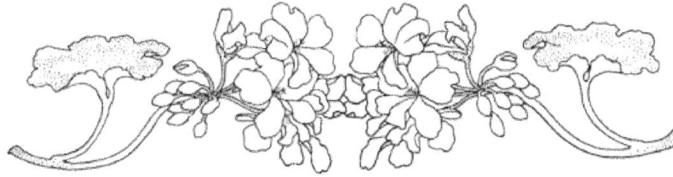

Virgin Most Powerful, pray for us.

Our Lady of the Miraculous Medal
November 27

"I knew nothing, I was nothing. For this reason God picked me."
—Catherine Labouré

On this Marian Feast we focus on the miraculous presence of Mary in our lives as *Virgin Most Powerful*. Thanks to a courageous and determined French woman, we celebrate this feast of *Our Lady of the Miraculous Medal* and have this treasured sacramental.

Catherine Labouré, at the age of 24, shortly after she completed caring for her father's household, entered the Sisters of Charity of St. Vincent de Paul at Chatillion-sur-Seine in France. While Catherine was preparing to become a nun, Our Lady appeared to her and gave her the vision for what would become known as the Miraculous Medal. Catherine told the story of her vision to her confessor, Father M. Aladel who, after many conversations, determined her story was genuine.

Catherine chose to remain anonymous throughout her life and only after she died in 1876 would there be an outburst of popularity towards her, as her visions and the medal were perceived as truly miraculous. One story tells of a twelve-year old girl who was completely healed of her physical disability while kneeling at Catherine's grave.

A devotion to the image of Our Lady under this title is rich with God's grace because of the very words spoken to Catherine by Our Lady, *"Have a medal struck on this model. All those who wear it will receive great graces. It should be worn around the neck. Great graces will be the portion of those who wear it with confidence."* Pope Pius XII declared Catherine Labouré a saint on July 27, 1947.

Teatime Chat

Because this feast falls right after Thanksgiving in the United States, plan on beginning your celebration with a prayer of thanksgiving to Our Lady. Invite everyone to share his or her gratitude to Mary and Jesus today. For what are they grateful? How about that she is the Mother of God!

Now, ask your children to think about what it would be like to receive a special message in person from Our Lady, as did St. Catherine Labouré. How would they feel? What would they do? Who would they tell? If, for example, they told someone, would they want others to know or would they want to remain anonymous like Catherine? Explain and discuss why it is important to pray with thanksgiving to God. By giving thanks to God and praising Him with our prayers, we grow closer to Him. We can ask Mary to deliver these prayers through our rosaries and simple daily prayers and offerings.

Psalm 34 provides a nice example of this kind of prayer.

I will bless the Lord at all times; his praise shall be ever in my mouth. Let my soul glory in the Lord; the lowly will hear me and be glad. Glorify the Lord with me, let us together extol his name. (Psalm 34:1-4)

As you read it, you might take this opportunity to explain how the Psalms were originally written as songs by King David and, as St. Augustine reminds us in his *Confessions,* singing is like praying twice. Also keep in mind that Mary prayed the Psalms all her life and we unite our prayers to hers when we pray with them.

Devotional Activities

♥ *Miraculous Accordion Prayer Booklets*

Supplies: Assorted cardstock, cereal boxes or cardboard, glue stick or craft glue, prayer cards, white printer paper, markers, crayons or colored pencils. Create lovely accordion books with some simple paper folding to make a beautiful prayer book for this feast! Because we are focusing on being thankful for this feast, our accordion books will reflect prayers of thanksgiving.

Directions: Follow the instructions at (www.makingbooks.com/accordion.shmtl). Use your materials to create a book of thanksgiving to *Our Lady of the Miraculous Medal.* A four panel accordion book would be lovely and your children can embellish them however they like to make them personalized and special!

♥ ***Order and distribute Miraculous medals*** to special friends and loved ones.

♥ ***Attend Mass*** and ask your priest to bless your medals.

> *"O Almighty and merciful God, Who, throughout the manifold apparitions of the Immaculate Virgin on earth, has deigned continually to perform wonderful things for the salvation of souls, graciously bestow Thy blessings on this medal, that they who piously venerate and devoutly wear it may feel Thy protection and obtain Thy mercy. Through Christ our Lord, amen. Our Lady of the Miraculous Medal, pray for us!"*
> —Traditional Blessing of a Miraculous Medal by a priest

♥ **Pray:** *A Decade of the Rosary*

Teatime Recipe Idea

Miraculous Medal Cookies

Bake oval shaped sugar cookies, frost white and decorate them with blue sugar sprinkles in the shape of the symbol found on the Miraculous Medal.

Miraculous Cocoa or Chocolate Milk

Hand your child a spoon and stir slowly as you pour hot (or cold) milk into mugs that already have chocolate syrup in them. Look! Chocolate milk miraculously appears!

Virgin Most Powerful, pray for us!

White Annunciation or Madonna Lily (Lilium candidum)

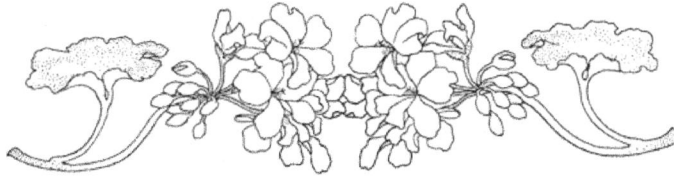

Virgin Most Merciful, pray for us.

Our Lady of Mercy
September 24

"For thus says the Lord God the Holy One of Israel: If you return and be quiet, you shall be saved: in silence and in hope shall your strength be."

—Isaiah 30:15

Today we celebrate the feast of Our Lady of Mercy as the *Virgin Most Merciful.* Because of the tenderness of Our Lady, she is considered our most merciful Mother. Her heart is so full of compassion that she uses her influence with God to petition for our salvation through his grace and mercy.

We as Christians call out to Mary, *"Hail holy queen, mother of mercy, our life, our sweetness and our hope . . ."* It is right for the faithful to address Mary in their time of need and seek her out for solace in our repentance and distress. For our God is a God of compassion and He planned for the salvation of our souls through His merciful and gracious mother.

Teatime Chat

During the *Wedding Feast at Cana* (John 2:1-12) Mary had compassion on the new bride and groom and gently urged Jesus to perform his miraculous changing of the water into wine as a work of mercy to the new couple. Even though Jesus said that his time had not yet come, Mary advocated for the new couple and thus showed her trust and confidence in God through his mercy. "Do whatever he tells you" (John 2:5).

Mary's mercy is so great because she has a clear understanding of the misery of every man, woman and child, after all, she is also known as *Our*

Lady of Sorrows. As a loving mother she wants to offer us the mercy of God! Mary took God's call as an act of compassion for humankind, she fulfilled God's will perfectly. Therefore she is a perfect example for us to follow. Our Lady's maternal mercy is like a salve on our open wounds. She is the mother of mercy, as Christ is Divine Mercy.

Devotional Activities

♥ *Act of Contrition Bookmarks*

Supplies: Cardstock in various colors or patterns cut about 2 ½ inches by 6-8 inches. Hole punch, ribbon or yarn, stickers, holy cards, colored pencils or markers.

Directions: Have your children hand copy the act of contrition prayer, or make photocopies for them to fit a desired size for a bookmark. Use the beautiful papers or cardstock and decorate as desired with stickers, holy cards, and ribbons, laminate for durability and keepsake, hole punch at the center top after laminating and insert the ribbon or yarn.

♥ *Attend Confession and Mass*

♥ Pray: *Divine Mercy Chaplet*

> *"O Lady, who can lack confidence in you, since you help even those who are in despair? And I have not the least doubt that, when we run to you, we shall obtain all we desire. Let those who have no hope, hope in you."*
>
> —*St. Bernard of Clairvaux d. 1153*

Teatime Recipe Idea

Merciful Blueberry Muffins

1 ¾ c	cake flour	¼ c	sour cream
2 t	baking soda	1 stick	unsalted butter, room temperature
1 t	cream of tartar		
1 t	salt	⅔ c.	butter
1 pint	fresh blueberries	1 large egg, room temperature	
¾ c	milk	1 large egg yolk, room temperature	

Directions: Preheat oven to 425°F. Butter or spray 18 muffin cups or line them with paper baking cups. Sift together the cake flour, soda, salt, and cream of tartar, twice. Remove a tablespoon or two of the dry ingredients to toss with the blueberries. In a separate bowl, stir the milk and sour cream together and set aside until needed.

In a mixer fitted with the paddle attachment, beat the butter on medium speed until white and pale, about 3 minutes. Add the sugar and beat until the mixture no longer feels grainy, about 3 minutes, scrape down the paddle and the sides of the bowl as needed. Add the eggs and yolk and beat until the mixture if fluffy, about 2 to 3 minutes.

Remove the bowl from the mixer and sift half of the dry ingredients into the bowl, add half of the mild and sour cream mixture and fold gently together, stopping when barely combined. Add the remaining dry and liquid mixtures and fold again just until combined. Sprinkle over the blueberries and barely fold them in as well.

Spoon the batter into the prepared muffin tins, filling each cup at least two-thirds full and bake for 18 to 20 minutes or until the tops, which will be flat, are golden and spring back when lightly pressed. Turn out onto a cooling rack and let cool for 10 to 15 minutes before serving. Enjoy with fresh strawberries and cream for a deliciously merciful treat!

Virgin Most Merciful, pray for us!

Zinnia
Religious Name: The Virgin

54

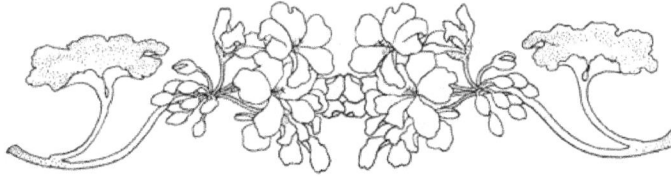

Virgin Most Faithful, pray for us.

The Visitation of the Blessed Virgin Mary
to her Cousin Elizabeth
May 31

"Shout for joy, O daughter Zion! Sing joyfully, O Israel! Be glad and exult with all your heart, O daughter Jerusalem…the Lord is in your midst." —Zephaniah 3:14-15

Today we celebrate the Feast of The Visitation of the Blessed Virgin to her cousin Elizabeth. As *Virgin Most Faithful* we will recall how Mary in her great love and generous spirit went to tend her kin. As she listened to the words of the Angel Gabriel at the *Annunciation*, she learned that Elizabeth too was with child, she went in haste to see her.

Upon arriving at her cousin's home in the hill country of Nazareth, Mary greets Elizabeth who is in her sixth month of pregnancy. A woman who was thought to be barren as was Sarah in the Old Testament (Genesis 18:9-15), she had been truly blessed by God with a child late in life. As Elizabeth exclaims, "And how is it that the Mother of my Lord should come to me?" (Luke 1:43) Mary thus answers her, "My soul doth magnify the Lord" (Luke 1:46). The utterance of these words have become known as *The Magnificat* or the *Canticle of the Blessed Virgin Mary* and comes from the beginning of the Latin text *Magnificat anima mea Dominum* which means *"my soul doth magnify the Lord."* They are Mary's own words and it is a prayer of praise to God for fulfilling his promise to her at the incarnation.

"That is why the Canticle of Mary, the Magnificat (Latin) or Megalynei (Byzantine) is the song both of the Mother of God and of the Church; the song of the Daughter of Zion and of the new

People of God; the song of thanksgiving for the fullness of graces poured out in the economy of salvation and the song of the "poor" whose hope is met by the fulfillment of the promises made to our ancestors, "to Abraham and to his posterity for ever."

—CCC 2619

Teatime Chat

This is a day to spend contemplating Our Lady rushing off to help her already very pregnant cousin Elizabeth in the hill country. Elizabeth would soon become the mother of John the Baptist who would pave the way for Jesus' teaching life. Mary as a helpmate to Elizabeth came to her aid, just when it would be evident to Elizabeth that she too was with child. As you relate the story of the *Visitation* to your children, I hope you will find it in your heart today to think of someone that might need your assistance and a little companionship even if in mind and soul, it is a beautiful way to share some gifts of the Holy Spirit and the best way to finish out this "Merry" Month of May.

The violet is considered a symbol of Mary's great humility and it would be appropriate to explain how Mary's constancy and innocence helped her throughout her life and how with humility she endured all of the joy and sorrow that would come with being the Mother of Jesus.

Have fun talking about teatime manners and hospitality today. One of our favorite books on the subject of manners is *Everyday Graces* by Karen Santorum (Delaware, ISI Books, 2003). Invoke Mary in her humility as you all pray a decade of the second Joyful rosary mystery in honor of the Visitation.

Devotional Activities

♥ *Spiritual Bouquets*

Special Note: If you can make this day into a field trip, preparing spiritual bouquets to deliver to a friend or someone in need would be a good example of humility and charity. Alternatively, you can work on your Spiritual Bouquets to deliver on a different day, like after Mass on Sunday.

Supplies: Selection of plain or decorative papers, ribbon, markers or pens, colored pencils, stickers and a special bible verse or Marian prayer to copy. (It can be as simple as the beginning lines of the *Magnificat*, or even something shorter).

Directions: Have your children choose from the craft supplies and let them set to work creating a special bouquet on paper (drawing flowers is *very* appropriate) and when finished, roll them into a scroll and tie them with a pretty ribbon to be delivered. These can be collected in a basket and placed near the Mary Altar until the day of delivery.

♥ **Memory or Copywork:** *The Magnificat* Your children may enjoy memorizing the *Magnificat* or alternatively using this beautiful verse to copy into a book or prayers or their Marian notebook or Scrapbook.

> *"My soul doth magnify the Lord. And my spirit hath rejoiced in God my Saviour. Because he hath regarded the humility of his handmaid; for behold from henceforth all generations shall call me blessed. Because he that is mighty, hath done great things to me; and holy is his name. And his mercy is from generation unto generations, to them that fear him. He hath showed might in his arm: he hath scattered the proud in the conceit of their heart. He hath put down the mighty from their seat, and hath exalted the humble. He hath filled the hungry with good things; and the rich he hath sent empty away. He hath received Israel his servant, being mindful of his mercy: As he spoke to our fathers, to Abraham and to his seed for ever."* —Luke 1:46-55

♥ **Poetry:** *Good and Bad Children*, Robert Louis Stevenson

♥ **Grace and Courtesy:** Have the children who are old enough serve tea to each other as a sign of hospitality and grace. If a younger can serve to an older child, this would be a very good lesson in grace and courtesy towards elders.

Teatime Recipe Idea

Tea Cake with Candied/Sugared Violets

1 ½ c	cake flour		2/3 c.	whole milk
¾ c	sugar		½ c	butter, softened
1½ t	baking powder		2	large eggs, lightly beaten
¼ t	salt		1½ t	pure vanilla extract

57

Directions: Preheat oven to 375°F. In a large mixing bowl, combine the flour, sugar, baking powder and salt. Add to this mixture the milk, softened butter, eggs and vanilla. Beat on low speed in an electric mixer until combined, then beat on medium for another minute. This step can also be done by hand. Pour the batter into a greased and floured 8" to 9" *spring form* pan or regular cake pan. Bake for approximately 25 minutes or until a wooden stick inserted into the center comes out clean and the top in golden brown. Let the cake cool on a wire rack for 15 minutes in the pan, and then remove the *spring form* sides and bottom and let cool completely on a plate. Dust with Confectioners' sugar and decorate the top and around the bottom of the cake (on the plate) with the Sugared Violets.

To make the Sugared Violets: You will need one bunch of violets, granulated sugar, one egg white, and a small paint brush.

Gather violets early in the day, or find them at the market (usually in the herb section). Whip the egg white until frothy. Working over a plate of granulated sugar, paint each violet with the egg white and carefully lay each violet in the sugar. Sprinkle more sugar on top and allow to dry on the plate. These lovely little treats can be used to decorate any dessert or used as a garnish on a plate of delicious items.

Virgin Most Faithful, pray for us!

Part 3

Marian Symbols

OUR LADY
SEAT OF WISDOM

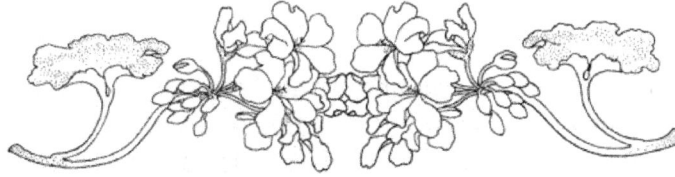

Mirror of Justice, pray for us.

Queen of the Apostles
Saturday after the Ascension of Our Lord

"You shall love your neighbor as yourself."
—Matthew 22:39

Mary is a model of love and kindness and she "mirrors" the image of God for us. She is the perfect model of justice as her whole life is a reflection of the love of God. We honor Mary as the Mirror of Justice in her title as *Queen of the Apostles* today. This is fitting as we have just celebrated the glorious feast of the *Ascension of Our Lord* and Mary is now reigning on earth for a time with the Apostles; she is truly a model of virtue for us today.

> *Let not your heart be troubled. You believe in God, believe also in me. In my Father's house there are many mansions. If not, I would have told you: because I go to prepare a place for you. And if I shall go, and prepare a place for you, I will come again, and will take you to myself; that where I am, you also may be…Jesus said to him: I am the way, and the truth, and the life. No man cometh to the Father, but by me.* —(John 14:1-6)

Mary understood well and practiced Jesus' teaching. (Matthew 16, 26) She has always mirrored the truth of the Father, even before she was born immaculate and pure. God has given Mary the fullness of His grace and made her truly the most blessed among women. In her humility, meekness, patience, mercy, faith, hope, purity and charity, she is the embodiment of the second most important commandment! Hopefully we can seek to imitate Mary and mirror some of God's truth for others in our lifetime as well.

Teatime Chat

Today is a good day to talk about the Apostles and what Mary's role must have been after Jesus ascended into heaven. Knowing that he was not coming again until the end of time, what must it have been like for those faithful left behind to do His work on earth? What help do you think Mary gave them? In what ways do you think Mary and the Apostles "mirrored" the truth of God?

The recipe for today includes *ganache,* which has a shiny silky look that resembles a mirror. Enjoy talking about all things "reflective" in regards to Our Lady as you enjoy this delicious and rich cake, fit for a Queen of Heaven!

Devotional Activities

♥ *Mirrored Tray Altars*

Supplies: Hot glue gun, small (unbreakable) mirrors sized to fit into a wooden tray.

Directions: After hot-gluing the mirror into the tray, decorate as a mini altar for Mary with a small statue, candle or votive some silk flowers in a vase or real if you have them and anything else you find appropriate for this lovely feast.

♥ *Apostles Creed prayer cards* ~ Copy the *Apostles Creed* sized about 2 ½ inches × 4 inches. Decorate and laminate for durability!

♥ Pray: *Rosary for the Crowning of Mary*

Acclamations in honor of the Mother of Christ

Mary the Dawn – Christ the Perfect Day;
Mary the Gate – Christ the Heavenly Way!
Mary the Root – Christ the Mystic Vine;
Mary the Grape – Christ the Sacred Wine!
Mary the Stem – Christ the Rose, blood-red;
Mary the Wheat – Christ the Living Bread!
Mary the Fount – Christ the Cleansing Flood;

Mary the Cup – Christ the Saving Blood!
Mary the Temple – Christ the Temple's Lord;
Mary the Shrine – Christ the God adored!
Mary the Beacon – Christ the heaven's Rest;
Mary the Mirror – Christ the Vision Blest!
Mary the Mother – Christ the Mother's Son;
By all things bless'd while endless ages run!
—Carmelite Prayer

Teatime Recipe Idea

Chocolate Ganache Cake

For the Cake -

2	sticks unsalted butter, softened
1 c	sugar
4	extra large eggs, room temperature
1	16 oz. can Hershey's chocolate syrup
1 T	pure vanilla extract
1 c	all purpose flour

For the Ganache –

½ c	heavy cream
8 oz.	semisweet chocolate chips
1 t	instant coffee granules optional

Directions: Preheat oven to 325°F. Butter and flour an 8-inch round cake pan lined with parchment paper, or alternatively use an 8-inch *spring form* pan. Cream the butter and sugar together until light and fluffy. Add the eggs, one at a time, mixing after each addition. Mix in the chocolate syrup and vanilla. Add the flour and mix until just combined. Be careful not to over beat or the cake will be tough. Pour the batter into the pan and bake for 40 to 45 minutes, or until just set in the middle. Let cool thoroughly in the pan.

For the *ganache*, cook the heavy cream, chocolate chips, and coffee granules in the top of a double boiler over simmering water until smooth and warm, stirring occasionally. Place the cake upside down on a wire rack situated on a cookie sheet and pour the ganache over the cake evenly. Make sure to cover both the cake and sides. You can tilt the rack to smooth the glaze. Serve immediately. You could also decorate with shiny silver *dragees* that can be found at cake decorating or craft stores!

Mirror of Justice, pray for us!

Venus Looking Glass, Our Lady's Mirror

64

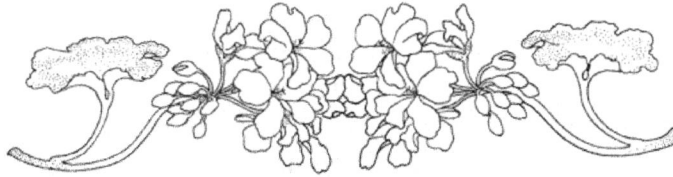

Seat of Wisdom, pray for us.

Mother of Divine Providence
Saturday before the 3rd Sunday of November

"Two ways there are, one of life and one of death, and there is a great difference between the two ways." —The Didache

The Blessed Virgin Mary is the only being found worthy to conceive and give birth to Eternal Wisdom, that is Our Lord Jesus Christ. Mary is the *Seat of Wisdom* because the Son of God, who lived in her womb, is eternal Wisdom. Because Mary begat and held the Son of God, she will lead us to a treasure more Holy than we can imagine, the Kingdom of Heaven. Mary obediently answered God's call when the angel Gabriel came to her, she conquered Eve's sin and thus her wisdom is a blessing to us all. Our Lady is an aid to our understanding of the eternal wisdom of God as she takes our petitions to Him. In His mercy He hears us and we strive to be ever faithful.

> *The seven gifts of the Holy Spirit are wisdom, understanding, counsel, fortitude, knowledge, piety, and fear of the Lord. They belong in their fullness to Christ, Son of David. (Isaiah 11:1-2) They complete and perfect the virtues of those who receive them. They make the faithful docile in readily obeying divine inspirations.* —CCC 1831

Teatime Chat

First discuss the idea of Mary as the *Seat of Wisdom*. What do we mean by someone or something being the "seat" of something? Consider this quote from Cardinal J. H. Newman:

Mary has this title in her Litany, because the Son of God, who is also called in Scripture the Word and Wisdom of God, once dwelt in her, and then, after His birth of her, was carried in her arms and seated in her lap in His first years. Thus, being as it were, the human throne of Him who reigns in heaven, she is called the "Seat of Wisdom." In the poet's words:

> His throne, thy bosom blest,
> O Mother undefiled.
> That Throne, if aught beneath the skies,
> Beseems the sinless Child.
>> (http://www.ewtn.com/library/MARY/SEATWISD.htm
>> Accessed May 20, 2012)

Then discuss the meaning of "providence" with your children. Here is the definition of it from the Catholic Encyclopedia:

> Providence in general, or foresight, is a function of the virtue of prudence, and may be defined as the practical reason, adapting means to an end. As applied to God, Providence is God Himself considered in that act by which in His wisdom He so orders all events within the universe that the end for which it was created may be realized. That end is that all creatures should manifest the glory of God, and in particular that man should glorify Him, recognizing in nature the work of His hand, serving Him in obedience and love, and thereby attaining to the full development of his nature and to eternal happiness in God. (http://www.newadvent.org/cathen/12510a.htm)

Mary was prepared to be the mother of Christ through God's Providence and she prays for us to Him that He may continue to provide for all we need. She is our spiritual mother in a very real sense.

Think of the divinity of God and the perfection of Our Lady as you enjoy this luscious treat today! Divinity can usually be found in the bakery section of most grocers, but it is much more fun to make your own! Everyone can learn the beautiful *Divine Praises* provided below.

Devotional Activities

♥ *Scripture Scrolls from the Book of Wisdom*

Supplies: Cream colored parchment paper or scrapbook paper in a light color, ¼ inch black satin ribbon, ¼ inch dowel cut pieces about 6-8 inches for each child.

Directions: Help your child select some beautiful scripture verses from the *Book of Wisdom*. Keep it simple and choose only a few lines or a short paragraph. Copy onto beautiful papers and roll up scroll style. You can even use small dowels cut to the size of your paper to further create a scroll like look. (Chopsticks will work in a pinch) ☺

> *"Wisdom sings her own praises, before her own people she proclaims her glory; in the assembly of the Most High she opens her mouth, in the presence of his hosts she declares her worth."* —Sirach 24: 1-2

♥ *Pray the Divine Praises*

Blessed be God.
Blessed be His Holy Name.
Blessed be Jesus Christ, true God and true man.
Blessed be the name of Jesus.
Blessed be His Most Sacred Heart.
Blessed be Jesus in the Most Holy Sacrament of the Altar.
Blessed be the Holy Spirit, the paraclete.
Blessed be the great Mother of God, Mary most holy.
Blessed be her holy and Immaculate Conception.
Blessed be her glorious Assumption.
Blessed be the name of Mary, Virgin and Mother.
Blessed be Saint Joseph, her most chaste spouse.
Blessed be God in His angels and in His Saints.

May the heart of Jesus, in the Most Blessed Sacrament, be praised, adored, and loved with grateful affection, at every moment, in all the tabernacles of the world, even to the end of time. Amen.

Teatime Recipe Idea

Divinity Candy

½ c	granulated sugar		½ c	water
¼ t	salt		2	large egg whites, room temp.
½ c	light corn syrup		1 t	vanilla extract

Directions: Be sure to make divinity on a dry day; candy will not harden on a humid day. In a medium saucepan over medium high heat, heat sugar, salt, syrup and water to boiling, stirring constantly until sugar is dissolved. Set candy thermometer in place and continue cooking over medium low heat, not stirring, until the temperature reaches 266°F. When the temperature reaches 260°F beat the egg whites with electric mixer at high speed, until stiff peaks form. While beating, pour the hot syrup slowly into the egg whites. Beat for about 2 to 3 minutes, until mixture isn't glossy. Add vanilla and turn to low speed. Continue beating until the mixture holds its shape when dropped from a spoon. It will probably be too thick for the mixer at this point. With a lightly buttered teaspoon, drop onto waxed paper. Work as quickly as possible. If mixture gets too thick to work with, add a few drops of water. Let stand until dry. Store in tightly covered containers. Enjoy, it will be divine!

Seat of Wisdom, pray for us!

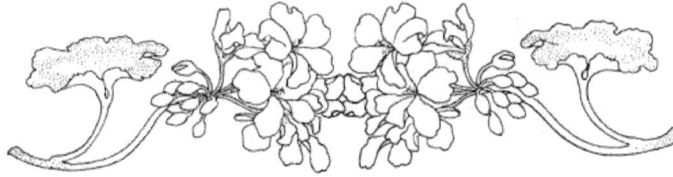

Cause of Our Joy, pray for us.

The Birth of the Blessed Virgin Mary
September 8

"The glorious stem of Jesse has brought forth an exquisite branch, from which has come forth a flower full of wondrous fragrance."
—Antiphon for the Memorial of Sts. Joachim and Anne, parents of the Blessed Virgin Mary, July 26

What a joy it is when a baby is born into the family! In recalling your own child's or children's births, you know just how special each one was and you again rejoice each time you celebrate them. I am sure that Sts. Joachim and Anne felt the same way when they remembered Mary's birth.

Today we honor Mary's birth and life as the new Eve and co-redemptrix in our salvation history. Mary's birth truly is the *Cause of Our Joy*. When we are joyful, we are able to look past our hurts and our faults and just be happy and today I am so happy to have a reason for a party in Mary's name!

Today we celebrate Mary as the *Cause of Our Joy* in her Immaculate Conception and birth. We are going to get a head start on our October devotion with a great visual reminder. Beginning today you will start the Mystical Rose Tree devotion (see *Mystical Rose* pg. 79) to be completed in time for the feast of *Our Lady of the Most Holy Rosary* on October 7. Much like the beautiful Marian candle you created for the feast of *Mary, Mother of God*, you will have something tangible to chart your growing love and faithfulness to the Blessed Virgin.

69

Every day or evening when you say your family rosary, and each time your children practice some devotion to Mary they may add a rose to the tree. Your hope is that by the end of September, your tree will be fairly bursting with roses for Mary and she will be so pleased to see your blossoming tree! (You can choose the length of time to spend on this, but from September 8 to October 7 allows a perfect amount of time for your tree to blossom with your daily devotions).

Teatime Chat

It would be fun to talk about your family's birthday celebration traditions and ask everyone what is their favorite part of the celebration, besides the presents. Today might be a good day for looking at scrapbooks or photos of family birthday celebrations and recalling how special each person's birthday is and what it means to be a child of God in His heavenly kingdom.

Devotional Activities

♥ Begin: *Tissue Paper Roses for Mystical Rose Tree*

Supplies: Assorted colors of tissue paper, green or tan pipe cleaners, clear tape and a display method.

Directions: Choose your method of display for your roses, perhaps a bare branch made from construction paper and taped to the wall or stickers on scrapbook paper for an 8 ½" × 11" notebook. Then begin to make tissue paper or origami roses and place them into a bowl or basket. If you would prefer to do this on paper or the wall, choose the appropriate size for your display space and the roses could either be hand-drawn by the children each time they complete a decade of the rosary or some other devotion, or you can tape tissue paper roses on accordingly. You can even use floral stickers.

♥ *Birthday Banner*

Supplies: Blue cardstock or floral scrapbook paper, scissors, ribbon or yarn.

Directions: Create a "Happy Birthday" banner for Mary using blue cardstock or floral scrapbook papers. Cut the paper into a pennant shape. Decorate with birthday greetings, hole-punch and thread with ribbon to hang over your table, altar or a window to show Mary your devotion to her in her birth all month long!

♥ **Sing:** *Happy birthday to Mary*

♥ **Pray:** *The Joyful Mysteries*

♥ **Recite:** *Litany of Loreto* in honor of Our Lady's birth and the whole reason for your celebration today, as she truly is the *Cause of Our Joy*!

Teatime Recipe Idea

Birthday Cake or Cupcakes – don't forget the candles!

Homemade Lemonade would be especially tasty for your beverage. Here is an easy recipe we have enjoyed:

Homemade Lemonade

| 3 ½ c | water | 2 c | fresh lemon juice (squeezed |
| 1 ½ c | sugar | | from about 10 large lemons) |

Directions: Bring water and sugar to a boil in a small saucepan, stirring occasionally until sugar dissolves. Let cool. Mix sugar syrup and lemon juice in a tall pitcher and stir to combine. Taste for tartness. If too tart, make some more syrup, or add a little honey to sweeten. Makes approximately 6 cups. Enjoy.

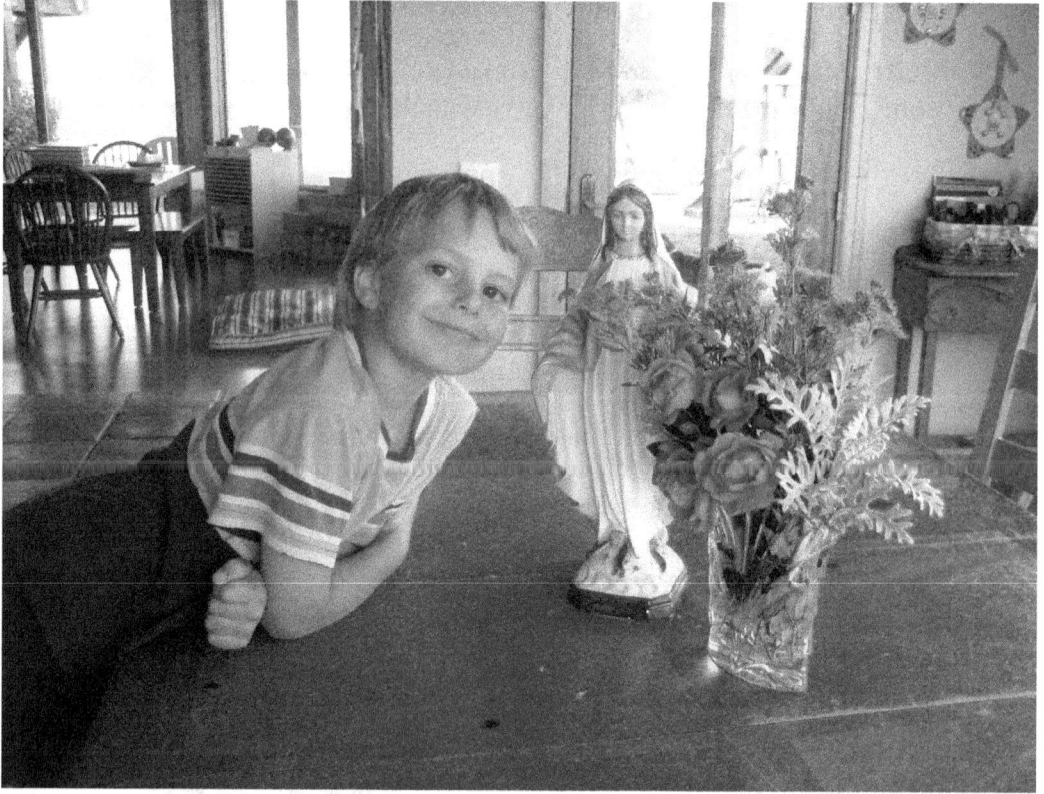

Cause of Our Joy, pray for us!

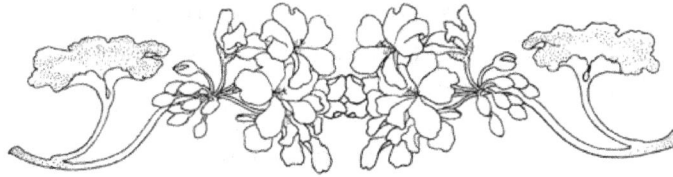

Spiritual Vessel, Vessel of Honor, Singular Vessel of Devotion

Our Lady of Mount Carmel, pray for us.
July 16

"I lift my eyes toward the mountains: whence shall help come to me? My help is from the Lord, who made heaven and earth."
—Psalm 121:1-2

The feast of Our Lady of Mount Carmel is a summer time feast instituted in the fourteenth century by the Carmelite Order. We will honor Mary in a trio of symbolic titles today as *Spiritual Vessel, Vessel of Honor* and *Singular Vessel of Devotion*. They represent the Blessed Mother as a vessel (container) of holiness, goodness, and grace.

This feast also reminds us of the devotion to the Brown Scapular as revealed by Our Lady to Saint Simon Stock back in the thirteenth century. Our Lady made known to him the benefits and graces that would be bestowed upon anyone who wears this sacramental in her honor when she said to him, *"Whosoever dies wearing this Scapular shall not suffer eternal fire"* (Mary's Promise made July 16, 1251 to St. Simon Stock). The small brown piece of wool cloth used today recalls the intention of being clothed in the garments of salvation and that of putting on Mary's attitudes and grace. This scapular became a signal of grace for the Carmelite order. And as mentioned above, Mary promised that whoever died in it would not suffer everlasting punishment and would quickly be released from purgatory. According to some scholars it has become one of the most widely practiced Marian devotion today next to wearing the Miraculous Medal.

The relation between Our Lady and Mount Carmel is geographic and biblical. Mount Carmel is about twenty miles from Nazareth and overlooks the Mediterranean Sea. It was considered a symbol of blessing and beauty for its rich vegetation, and a place of sacred memory to recall the second covenant between God and Israel.

Mount Carmel eventually attracted hermits, and from the twelfth century on, those in residence officially became known as the *Brothers of the Blessed Virgin Mary of Mount Carmel.* Following in the footsteps of Mary they developed a Marian spirituality that is still in full practice and devotion today and was formally approved at the Council of Lyon in 1274. Modern day Carmelites include St. Teresa of Avila and St. Theresa Benedicta of the Cross (Edith Stein).

> *The voice of one crying in the desert: Prepare ye the way of the Lord, make straight in the wilderness the paths of our God. Every valley shall be exalted, and every mountain and hill shall be made low, and the crooked shall become straight, and the rough ways plain. And the glory of the Lord shall be revealed, and all flesh together shall see, that the mouth of the Lord hath spoken.* (Isaiah 40:3-5)

Teatime Chat

Read aloud I Kings 18: 41-46 to your children today and you will hear about how the prophet Elijah prayed at Mount Carmel for rain, which was announced by a little cloud rising from the sea. The little cloud was subsequently identified as a symbol for Mary and eventually developed into the title *Star of the Sea* (see Part 3, The Symbolic Mary).

I love that wearing a brown scapular helps us to recall the *intention* of being clothed in the garments of salvation and that of putting on Mary's attitudes and her grace. Oh, how much nicer the world would be if we all did this! The Carmelite *ideal* lends perfectly for your devotion of Mary today.

Mary is considered a *Singular Vessel of devotion*, honor and love created by God to bring Our Lord into the world. The symbolism of a *vessel* used for Mary can be many things. A vessel is used to carry water or grain and thus Mary *as* a vessel brought Jesus into the world who would be the bread of life for us in the Eucharist and the living water of our baptisms. She is this *Singular Vessel* of holiness as no one is closer to Jesus than Mary, and she wants us to be closer to him as well.

How then can we grow closer to Jesus? With our reverent devotion to Mary, we can ask her as *Spiritual Vessel* to take our prayers right to Our Lord. It is really quite that simple!

Devotional Activities

♥ Make or purchase **Brown Scapulars** and present them to your children today.

♥ *Our Lady of Mt. Carmel Holy Card Stands*

Supplies: Bag of Caramel squares, toothpicks or plastic cocktail spears, holy cards of Our Lady of Mt. Carmel, tape, paper doily or plate to build on.

Directions: Let your children build a tower or mountain with some of the caramel squares. Tape a toothpick or cocktail spear to the back of a holy card then insert through the top caramel square of each mountain. Make sure you discard the towers or mountains after a few days of being displayed, as they will become very hard and not edible. **Please also note that this craft may not be suitable for children under 3 due to the small and chewy nature of the caramel squares may pose a choking hazard.*

♥ **Pray:** *Prayer to Our Lady of Mount Carmel*

> *O beautiful flower of Carmel, most fruitful vine, Splendor of Heaven, Holy and singular, who brought forth the Son of God, still ever remaining a Pure Virgin, assist me in this necessity. O Star of the Sea, help and protect me! Show me that Thou art my Mother! O Mary, conceived without sin, pray for us who have recourse to thee!*
>
> *Mother and Ornament of Carmel, Pray for us!*
> *Virgin, Flower of Carmel, Pray for us!*
> *Patroness of all who wear the Scapular, Pray for us!*
> *Hope of all who die wearing the Scapular, Pray for us!*
> *St. Joseph, Friend of the Sacred Heart, Pray for us!*
> *St. Joseph, Caste Spouse of Mary, Pray for us!*
> *St. Joseph, Our Patron, Pray for us!*
> *O sweet Heart of Mary, Be our Salvation!*
> —Prayer of St. Simon Stock, known as the Flos Carmeli

Teatime Recipe Idea

Ice Cream Mountains with Carmel Sauce and Clouds of Cream

Serve mounded vanilla ice cream and drizzle with warmed caramel sauce and top with a cloud of whipped cream. The whip cream and caramel can be store bought or here is a delectable recipe for caramel, so good you have to try it at least once.

For the Caramel:

1 ½ c	sugar	Optional:
1 ¼ c	heavy cream	chopped pecans
½ t	pure vanilla extract	to sprinkle on
		top!

Directions: Mix 1/3 c. water and the sugar in a medium heavy-bottomed saucepan. Cook without stirring, over low heat for 5 to 10 minutes, until sugar dissolves. Increase the heat to medium and boil uncovered until the sugar turns a warm chestnut brown color (about 350°F on a candy thermometer), 5 to 8 minutes, gently swirling the pan to stir the mixture. Be careful; the mixture is extremely hot! Watch it constantly at the end, as it will go from caramel to burned very quickly. Turn of the heat. Slowly add the cream, and be extra careful of spatters, then add the vanilla. The cream will bubble vigorously and the caramel will solidify; simmer over low heat, stirring constantly until the caramel dissolves and is smooth, about 2 to 3 minutes. Allow sauce to cool to room temperature, and it will thicken as it sits in about 2 to 3 hours.

Spiritual Vessel, Vessel of Honor,
Singular Vessel of Devotion, pray for us!

Rosa

78

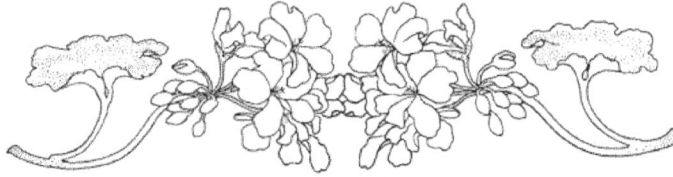

Mystical Rose, pray for us.

Our Lady of the Most Holy Rosary
October 7

*"I am a flower of Sharon, a lily of the valley. As a lily among thorns, so is my beloved among women." —*Song of Songs 2:1-2

We honor Mary today on this feast of Our Lady of the Most Holy Rosary in her symbolic title of *Mystical Rose*. In fact, the entire month of October has been dedicated to Mary and the devotion to the Rosary, so you may already be well acquainted with this devotion.

The Rosary, above all other Marian devotions, is the most well known form of prayer to Our Lady and yet sometimes the most dismissed as trivial. Many graces can be obtained from our Blessed Mother by asking for her prayers in the Rosary.

Even the smallest of children can learn the Hail Mary by heart when heard repeatedly each day.

Hail Mary, full of grace, the Lord is with you. Blessed art thou among women and blessed is the fruit of your womb. Holy Mary, Mother of God, pray for us sinners, now and at the hour of our death. Amen.

Because we are celebrating the symbolic today, we look to God's creation. Mary has been symbolized with flowers over the centuries and what makes this intriguing is that it gives vivid evidence of Mary's presence in our lives. All around us flowers bloom, we only have to look outside at God's goodness in nature and there you will see Mary reflected in the flowers. It is no wonder that he used the rose to take the place of His mother and queen when speaking of her and the love she has for us poor sinners in the world. In fact almost all flowers can be attributed to Our Lady in some way (see the feast of *Our Lady of Sorrows*, page 121).

> *You are a garden fountain, a well of water flowing fresh from Lebanon. Arise, north wind! Come, south wind! Blow upon my garden that its perfumes may spread abroad. My lover has come down to his garden, to the beds of spice, To browse in the garden and to gather lilies. —Song of Songs 4:15-16, 6:2b*

Teatime Chat

*Special Note: If you have already celebrated Mary's birthday on September 8, you have been working hard on your devotions and prayers and adding to your Mystical Rose tree. By the time we come to this feast you will have a tree fairly bursting with roses for Our Lady.

All your hard work since Our Lady's birthday has paid off! This will truly be a welcoming sight for you and your children as leaves are falling from the trees outside, you will have created a beautiful blossoming tree for Mary inside. The tissue paper roses are a constant reminder of the presents you gave to Jesus and Mary each time you followed through on your devotions and prayers. Whenever you added a rose to your tree, you sent a message of love to Jesus *through* His Mother.

During Advent, our family read the picture book *The Donkey's Dream* by Helen Berger and recalled some of Mary's titles in this symbolic telling of the nativity story. If you choose to share this book with your children today, explain how Mary as *Mystical Rose* is part of our lives everyday. And that each time you prayed a *Hail Mary* or said your rosary, you gave Mary another rose for her Heavenly garden.

Devotional Activities

♥ *Single Mystery Rosaries*, otherwise known as "sacrifice beads" (**Special Note: order these one decade rosary kits from www.thelittleways.com one month in advance).

Making rosaries is a delightful and fun activity for children of all ages. Even the littlest can help you string beads to create a lovely handmade keepsake for this special feast.

Supplies & Directions: Rosary kits, or your own rosary-making supplies, including 11 beads each, rosary cording, a crucifix, a medal of your choice or a miraculous medal, scissors. Create your own design for one-decade rosaries using beads you may already have on hand. Visit: www.olrm.org (Our Lady's Rosary Makers for free instructions)

♥ *Assemble the Mystical Rose Basket Cupcakes* (if you are having teatime)

♥ **Pray:** *Rosary to Our Lady as Mystical Rose*

♥ **Sing:** *Bring Flowers of the Rarest*

Teatime Recipe Idea

Mystical Rose Basket Cupcakes

Baked cupcakes (any flavor you desire) white frosting , red fruit leather or roll-ups shaped into roses

red rope licorice (for basket handle) coconut pre-colored green (you can do this in a zip-topped bag with a few drops of green food coloring, shake to mix)

Directions: Assemble and enjoy with rose red fruit punch in pretty glasses or teacups! See photo below for an example, have fun!

Mystical Rose, pray for us!

Our Lady of Knock

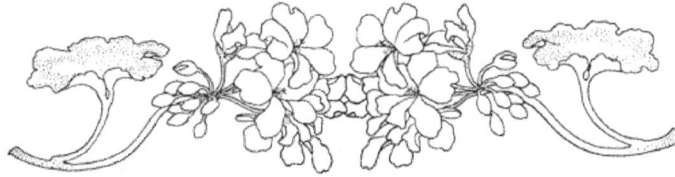

Tower of David, pray for us.

Our Lady of Knock
August 21

"Only a fool would fail to praise God in his might, when the tiny mindless birds praise him in their flight." —Early Irish Blessing

We celebrate Our Lady today as *Tower of David* and for her special devotion to the faithful at Ireland's revered Marian Shrine in County Mayo dedicated to *Our Lady of Knock Ireland*. An approved apparition of Our Lady took place there in 1879. According to Zsolt Aradi, in his book *Shrines to Our Lady Around the World* (Farrar, Straus, and Young, 1954):

> On August 21, 1879, the figures of Mary, Joseph, and John the Apostle appeared over the gable of the village church in Knock Ireland. The church was enveloped in a bright light. Beside the figures there was an altar, with a cross on it and a lamb at its feet. None of the figures spoke any words at all. The parish priest was informed the next day, as he would not come out despite the pleas of the onlookers. They were also too amazed to leave the scene. Twice in 1880 the apparition was repeated, but the light was too intense to clearly recognize anyone but Mary. (pp. 99-102)

Mary is revered as *Tower of David* in her solid and rock-like devotion to her Son. She banished all evil from the moment of her birth and continues to provide a tower of mercy and refuge for all on earth.

Teatime Chat

There is great devotion to this beautiful Lady in Ireland as well as worldwide. She is considered *Our Lady of Silence*, as during these apparitions at Knock she spoke no words, only gazed upward toward heaven. Perhaps today is the day for some silent reflection time during your teatime! What are some ways you like to spend quiet time in prayer? An area in each child's room or a special corner of the house can easily be set up as a prayer corner for quiet contemplation time. Do not forget to place a few of your favorite prayer books and a statue of Mary.

Irish Soda Bread is not just for St. Patrick's Day, bake up a batch of this delicious bread and enjoy a lovely tea honoring Mary in this special title!

Hail Mary in Gaelic

> *"Sé do bheath' a Mhuire, atá lán de ghrásta, tá an Tiarna leat.*
> *Is beannaithe thú idir mná agus is beannaithe toradh do bhruinne Iosa.*
> *A Naomh Mhuire, a mháthair Dé, guí orainn na peacaithe, anois is ar*
> *uair ar mbás." Amen.*

Devotional Activities

♥ Litany of Knock Prayer Cards

Supplies: Reduced copies of the *Litany of Our Lady of Knock* for each child (old enough to read) sized to fit onto a bookmark or prayer card and hand them out for decorating. You may like to have stickers and stamps out for this, or simply markers, crayons or colored pencils, scissors, glue sticks.

Directions: Glue the Litany onto a bookmark or prayer card sized cardstock and embellish as desired. Pray the Litany together at teatime or after your evening meal. It would be fun to do this outside just after dusk with candles!

Litany of Our Lady of Knock

Great Mary,
Greatest of Mary's,
Greatest of Women,
Mother of Eternal Glory,
Mother of the Golden Light,
Honor of the Sky,
Temple of the Divinity,
Fountain of the Gardens,
Serene as the Moon,
Bright as the Sun,

Garden Enclosed,
Temple of the Living God,
Light of Nazareth,
Beauty of the World,
Queen of Life,
Ladder of Heaven,
Mother of God.

Pray for us.

—Eleventh Century Irish Litany of Mary

♥ *Lambs for Our Lady of Knock*

Supplies: Cotton or wool felt balls, glue stick, cardstock or paper plate, thin and stretchy rubber bands, black or pink construction paper.

Directions: Cut cardstock into a lamb shape and glue cotton (or other) balls over all to create a fluffy lamb. Or alternatively create a lamb face mask with the paper plate hole punching on either side of the face to insert the rubber band for a head band. Cut out and glue on lamb ears to the upper sides. Wear and enjoy!

♥ Print and Display: Please feel free to copy and cut out this Celtic Cross for your feast today. A Simple mobile could easily be created for a hanging centerpiece.

♥ Pray:

Our Lady of Knock, Queen of Ireland, you gave hope to our people in a time of distress and comforted them in sorrow. You have inspired countless pilgrims to pray with confidence to your divine Son, remembering His promise: "Ask and you shall receive, Seek and you shall find." Help me to remember that we are all pilgrims on the road to heaven. Fill me with love and concern for my brothers and sisters in Christ, especially those who live with me. Comfort me when I am sick or lonely or depressed. Teach me how to take part ever more reverently in the holy Mass. Pray for me now, and at the hour of my death. Amen.

♥ **Research**: Discover the symbolism of Mary as Tower of David. You can read about it at this website:
http://campus.udayton.edu/mary/prayers/turrisdavidica.html

> *Your neck is the tower of David, a display of trophies, a thousand bucklers hang on it, all of them worn by heroes of war.*
> — *Song of Songs 4:4*

Teatime Recipe Idea

"Tower of David" Irish Soda Bread

4 c	unbleached all purpose flour	1 ½ t	kosher salt
1 t	baking soda	2 c	buttermilk

Directions: Preheat oven to 375°F. Grease an 8-inch iron skillet, a glass pie plate, or baking sheet and set aside. Mix the flour, baking soda, and salt into a bowl and stir to combine. Add the buttermilk and stir vigorously until the dough comes together. Then turn the dough out onto a lightly floured surface and gently knead for a minute. Do not overwork the dough as it will become tough. Pat the dough into a disk about 6 to 8 inches across and slash an "x" about ½ inch deep across the top. Place into your prepared baking pan and bake for about 50 minutes or until the bread is golden brown and the "x" has widened a bit. Transfer to a cooling rack, then slice and serve! It is most delectable served warm with a meal or tea. A funny note on storing if there is any leftover that by the end of the day it will be as hard as the "blarney stone" due to the tiny amount of fat in the buttermilk.

Tower of David, pray for us!

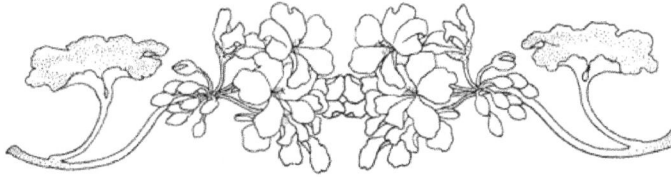

Tower of Ivory, pray for us.

Our Lady of the Snows
August 5

Let the cities of Judah rejoice, because of your judgments. Go about Zion, make the round; count her towers. Consider her ramparts, examine her castles, that you may tell a future generation that such is God, Our God forever and ever; he will guide us. —Psalm 48:12-15

Devotion to Mary under the title of Our Lady of the Snows is one of the oldest devotions to Mary. We will reverence Mary today in her symbolic title *Tower of Ivory*.

There is a legend about a marvelous snowfall in Rome in 352 A.D. Mary appeared in a dream to a rich but childless Roman couple that she wanted a church built in her honor and the location of the site would have a special sign from her. On a hot, sultry morning on August 5, Esquiline Hill was covered with snow. All the peoples of Rome proclaimed the summer snows a miracle, and a church to honor Mary was built on the hill six years later in 358 A.D. It has been restored and refurbished many times. This church, now known as the magnificent Basilica of St. Mary Major, still stands today as the seat of devotion to Our Lady of the Snows in the Catholic Church.

Saint Mary Major is the oldest church in the West dedicated to the Blessed Virgin Mary.

Teatime Chat

Wouldn't it be amazing to see snow in the summer? Perhaps creating your own shrine to Our Lady of the Snows would be a fun thing on a hot summers day. When thinking of Mary as a *Tower of Ivory*, there are many ways in which to devote oneself to Our Lady for this feast. Of course attending Mass would be perfect, but if that were not a possibility, might I suggest planting some lovely "snow in summer" in and around your Mary garden. If you do not have a set garden for Mary yet, try these adorable flower pots and tuck a tiny statue of Mary inside!

Devotional Activities

♥ *Snow in Summer flower pots*

Supplies: Small starts of Snow in Summer (*Cerastium*) for each child. Potting soil, one 3-5 inch terracotta pot for each child (or other small pots), one each small picture or holy card of Mary, craft paint, paint brushes, plastic spoons, newspaper or paper towels, glue stick, tooth pick or very small plant stake.

Directions: Give each child a pot, a plant start, some soil, plastic spoon, and holy card. Show them how to plant the pot out and stick the holy card of Mary into the soil either with a small plant stake, toothpick or affix to the side of the pot with a glue stick. This is a delightful little tiny flower is used mainly as a ground cover as it spreads rapidly. If you have a Mary garden already planted, then just add some of this delightful little plant and watch is spread. Remember to tuck in a small statue of Our Lady too if your pot is large enough. Water well and enjoy!

♥ *St. Mary Major Churches*

Supplies: Modeling clay or an unpainted small wood house.

Directions: Shape or paint as desired and dedicate to St. Mary Major in her title as *Our Lady of the Snows*.

♥ *Scatter white rose petals* in honor of the "snow" of Our Lady

♥ Pray:

> *Lord, pardon the sins of your people. May the prayers of Mary, the mother of your Son, help to save us, for by ourselves we cannot please you. Grant this through our Lord Jesus Christ, your Son, who lives and reigns with you and the Holy Spirit, one God, forever and ever.*
> —*Opening prayer, Feast of Our Lady of the Snows*

♥ **Research** the symbolism as Mary as Tower of Ivory. You can read about it at this website:
http://campus.udayton.edu/mary/prayers/turriseburnea.html

Teatime Recipe Idea

Bake a batch of your favorite brownies and dust with powdered sugar, even better if you crumble them a bit to form a mountainside. Alternatively, whip up a batch of melt-in-your-mouth Snowballs, delicious! Here are two recipes to suit your fancy.

Favorite Brownies

½ c	butter	2 c	sugar
4 oz.	Unsweetened chocolate	1 t	vanilla extract
4	eggs, room temperature	1 c	sifted all-purpose flour
¼ t	salt		confectioners' sugar for garnish

Directions: Preheat oven to 350°F. Melt butter and chocolate in microwave or in a bowl over a simmering pan on the stove. Let mixture cool. Beat the eggs and salt until light yellow and gradually add the sugar and vanilla. Beat until well creamed. Combine the cooled chocolate mixture and the egg mixture and fold in the flour, stir until smooth. Pour into a greased 9 × 13-inch pan and bake for approximately 25 minutes. Do not over bake so the brownies remain chewy. Let cool before cutting. Enjoy with powdered sugar sprinkled on top!

Snowballs

1 c	butter	1 t	vanilla
½ c	powdered sugar	2 c	ground pecans
1 t	baking powder	2 c	flour

Directions: Mix all ingredients and refrigerate for an hour. Roll into balls and bake on a greased cookie sheet at 350°F for 15-18 minutes. While still hot from the oven roll in 2 cups powder sugar. Let cool and then roll again, enjoy!

Tower of Ivory, pray for us!

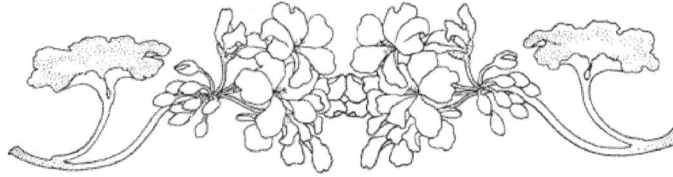

House of Gold, pray for us.

Our Lady of Guadalupe
December 12

Hear me and understand well, my son the least, that nothing should frighten or grieve you. Let not your heart be disturbed. Do not fear that sickness, nor any other sickness or anguish. Am I not here, who is your Mother? Are you not under my protection? Am I not your health? Are you not happily within my fold? What else do you wish? Do not grieve nor be disturbed by anything.
—Our Lady to Juan Diego, 1531

These words, as spoken by Mary to Juan Diego, would be the catalyst for change in the history of the people of Latin America. More people of Mexico were converted to Catholicism after the apparitions of Our Lady of Guadalupe to Juan Diego than any other apparition to date. We are forever grateful to this humble Indian man who encountered Our Lady on Mount Tepeyac and now we have this special devotion to Our Blessed Mother. We are going to celebrate Our Lady of Guadalupe today in her title as *House of Gold* in the *Litany of Loreto*.

A great sign appeared in the sky, a woman clothed with the sun, with the moon under her feet, and on her head a crown of twelve stars. —(Revelations 12: 1-2)

Teatime Chat

The symbolism for Our Lady of Guadalupe as *House of Gold* is rich with imagery. When Solomon built the Temple in Jerusalem, he wanted it to be made of the richest and best materials—like gold. After all, he expected God

91

to dwell there. Mary, as the symbolic House of Gold is made pure and immaculate to "house" the child Jesus.

Our Lady is a golden treasure trove of goodness, and as holy mother Church we represent her as such today. I think your children will have fun creating a house of gold for Mary.

If you have decided to read the Tomie de Paola book or watch the DVD ask the children what it would have been like to be Juan Diego and see Our Lady on the mountain so many times. Why do they think the Bishop questioned Juan Diego's story? It was extraordinary that Our Lady gave Juan Diego such a miraculous sign of the roses of Castile and her image on his Tilma!!

Devotional Activities

♥ *House of Gold shrines*

Supplies: Small wood house or framed shelf, gold wood or spray paint.

Directions: Spray or paint gold the small wooden house or shelf. Display a statue or holy card of Our Lady of Guadalupe with small vase of flowers.

♥ **Read:** *The Lady of Guadalupe,* by Tomie de Paola or watch the DVD *Juan Diego, Messenger of Guadalupe.*

♥ **Pray:**

> *Our Lady of Guadalupe, mystical rose, make intercession for Holy Church, protect the Sovereign Pontiff, help all those who invoke thee in their necessities, and since thou art the ever Virgin Mary and Mother of the true God, obtain for us from thy most holy Son the grace of keeping our faith, sweet hope in the midst of the bitterness of life, burning charity and the precious gift of final perseverance. Amen.*
> —Pope Pius X, 1950

Teatime Recipe Idea

Pie Crust Tilmas with Cinnamon Sugar

Directions: Purchase pre-made piecrusts in your refrigerator section at the grocery store. Cut into a "tilma" shape and brush with melted butter, then sprinkle with cinnamon sugar. Bake at 350°F for about 7-10 minutes or until golden brown. Let cool slightly before serving.

Other Mexican recipes

Favorite Flan

½ c	sugar		1	14 oz. can sweetened
3	Eggs			condensed milk
2 c	whole milk		1 T	vanilla extract

Directions: Preheat oven to 375°F; have ready a one-quart baking dish and a kettle of boiling water. Cook the sugar in a small, heavy pan over medium heat for several minutes, stirring constantly, until all the sugar melts and turns a golden brown. Be careful not to let it burn. Immediately pour the caramelized sugar into the baking dish and tilt the dish to coat the bottom and sides. Set aside.

In a large bowl, beat the remaining ingredients until well blended. Pour the mixture into the baking dish, right onto the caramelized sugar.

Place the baking dish in a larger pan on the middle rack of the oven. Pull the rack out far enough to fill the larger pan with an inch of boiling water. Slowly push the rack back in and bake for approximately 70 minutes, or until a knife inserted in the center of the custard comes out clean.

Let the flan cool for an hour, then cover with plastic wrap and refrigerate overnight. Before serving, run a knife around the outside edge of the flan to loosen it from the baking dish. Cover tightly with an inverted serving dish and turn over to unmold.

Mexican Hot Chocolate with Whipped Cream

½ c	sugar		4 c	milk
¼ c	Cocoa powder		¾ t	vanilla extract
Dash	salt		¼ t	cinnamon plus extra for
⅓ c	hot water			dusting the whipped cream

Directions for stovetop cocoa for six servings: Mix sugar, cocoa and salt in a saucepan, stir in hot water. Cook and stir over medium heat until mixture boils, boil and stir 2 minutes. Stir in milk and heat gently over low heat, do NOT BOIL again. Remove from heat, stir in vanilla and cinnamon. Pour into cups top with whipped cream and dust with cinnamon!

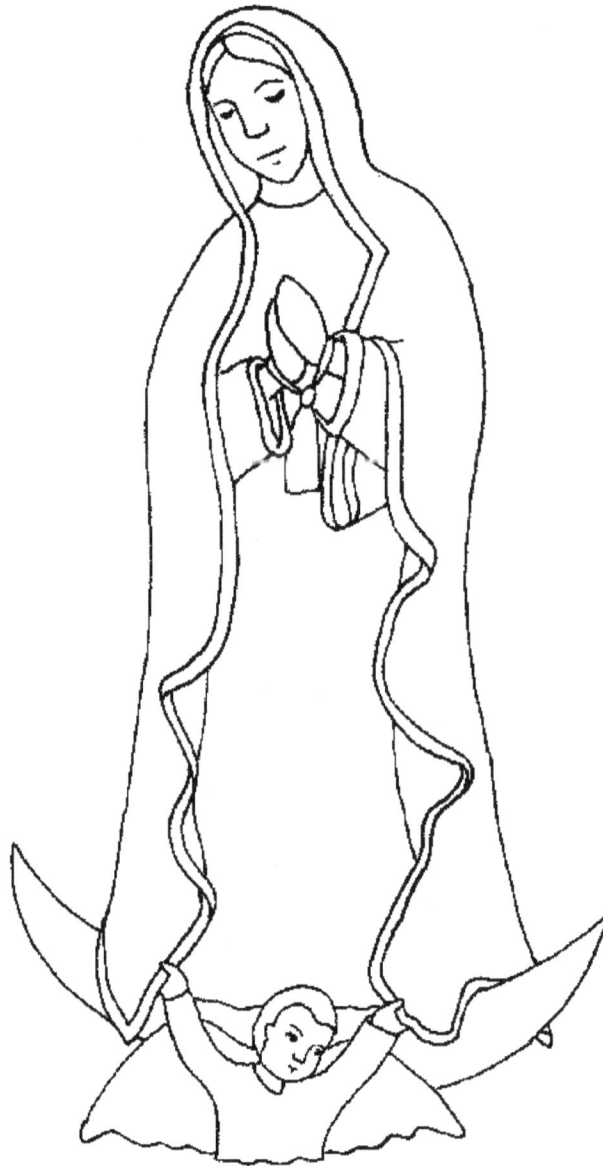

House of Gold, pray for us!

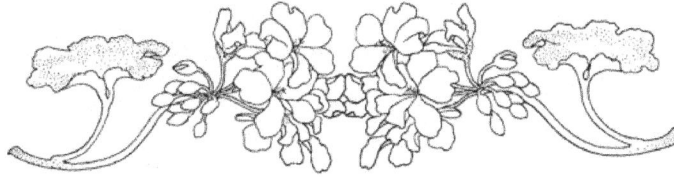

Ark of the Covenant, pray for us.

Our Lady of the Blessed Sacrament
May 13

In the Old Covenant bread and wine were offered in sacrifice among the first fruits of the earth as a sign of grateful acknowledgment to the Creator. But they also received a new significance in the context of the Exodus: the unleavened bread that Israel eats every year at Passover commemorates the haste of the departure that liberated them from Egypt; the remembrance of the manna in the desert will always recall to Israel that it lives by the bread of the Word of God (Deut 8:3) their daily bread is the fruit of the promised land, the pledge of God's faithfulness to his promises. The cup of blessing (1 Corinthians 10:16) at the end of the Jewish Passover meal adds to the festive joy of wine an eschatological dimension: the messianic expectation of the rebuilding of Jerusalem. When Jesus instituted the Eucharist, he gave a new and definitive meaning to the blessing of the bread and the cup. —CCC 1334*

The very first feast of Our Lady of the Blessed Sacrament in May of 1856 is possibly a foreshadowing of the appearance of *Our Lady of Fatima* of May 13, 1917. Mary as the Mother of Our Lord has the inherent virtue of faith in believing that Christ is truly present in the Eucharist. This too should be the center of our devotion, Our Eucharistic Lord, as He is grace and mercy. Mary's example of true adoration is something we should follow straight to the tabernacle to pray. This symbolic title for Mary in the *Litany of Loreto* images Mary as the *Ark of the new Covenant* that she will bring forth a new salvation for God's people.

"The Church renders devotion to our Lady in the Eucharist because Mary is joined by an inseparable bond to the saving work of her Son, which is made present in the Eucharist."
—The Greatest Marian Titles, Anthony Buono
(Alba House, 2008)

Because of this, the Church celebrates and honors Our Lady within the context of the church year liturgical cycle that is centered on the mysteries of Christ. What is of importance here is that we receive and adore Jesus in the Eucharist. We can give of ourselves to Jesus through His Mother at the sacrifice of the Mass. In imitation of Our Lady we are following her Son's commandments. Mary's joyous giving and loving contemplation are to be emulated as we seek perfection in Christ.

In the words of Saint Peter Julian Eymard, "Eucharistic adoration is the greatest of actions. To adore is to share the life of Mary on earth when she adored the Word Incarnate in her virginal womb, when she adored Him in the Crib, on Calvary, in the divine Eucharist." Source: http://www.therealpresence.org/eucharst/tes/quotes3.html
In Revelation 11:19-12:1 St. John tells us what he sees in Heaven:

> Then God's temple in heaven opened and in the temple could be seen the *ark of His covenant*. There were flashes of lightning, and peals of thundering, an earthquake, and a violent hailstorm. A great sign appeared in the sky, a woman clothed with the sun, with the moon under her feet, and on her head a crown of twelve stars. (Emphasis added.)

Teatime Chat

Bask in the beauty of Our Eucharistic Lord today. If you have never gone to Adoration before, it is a good day to introduce your children to this form of devotion of the church. Not to mention all the graces you will gain just by being present with Jesus in the Eucharist. If you are not able to give a Holy hour to Jesus, then try to model the concept to your children by setting up an altar with a tabernacle and sanctuary light and a quiet place for them to practice being present with Our Lord. Mary will be right there by your side the whole way!

Devotional Activities

♥ *Tabernacle & Sanctuary Light for Our Lord*

Supplies: small empty box with lid, 7" × 7" is a good size or a little larger, gold spray paint, or gold cellophane or wrapping paper, a Ciborium (please see Resource Appendix D), a sanctuary light or use red glass votives and candles.

Tabernacle Directions: If using the paint, spray the entire box and lid inside and out and let dry overnight if possible. If using wrapping paper or cellophane, cover the entire box and lid inside and out with the paper using double stick tape or craft glue. Using a craft knife or good kitchen shears, cut "doors" into the lid of the box. If you do not have a ciborium you can use a special silver dish or spray paint a plastic dish to represent the ciborium

♥ **Attend:** *Eucharistic Adoration* (known as a "Holy Hour" with Our Lord)

Pray the Spiritual Communion Prayer. You can print the prayer on nice card stock and have your child decorate it with a small holy card. Older children can copy the prayer.

> *My Jesus, I believe that You are present in the Most Holy Sacrament. I love You above all things, and I desire to receive You into my soul. Since I cannot at this moment receive You sacramentally, come at least spiritually into my heart. I embrace You as if You were already there and unite myself wholly to You. Never permit me to be separated from You.*

♥ **Pray:** *Novena to Our Lady of the Blessed Sacrament* found at

> http://tinyurl.com/MWM-novena1

♥ **Pray:** *Prayer to Our Lady after Holy Communion*

> *O my sweet Mother Mary, mother of Him Whom I hold within my heart, keep that heart which thy Jesus has chosen this day for His dwelling; defend it by thy ceaseless prayer, and obtain for me that the spirit of my Jesus, abiding with me, may continually remind me of the gift of gifts I have received and inflame my heart with love and with all holy desires.*
>
> *Pray for thy child, O dearest Mother, that the soul of him who has been a living tabernacle for the Eucharistic God may seek in all things the glory of that God and the interests of His Sacred Heart. Amen.*

Teatime Recipe Idea

Shortbread "Host" Cookies

3 sticks	unsalted butter, softened	3 ½ c	all purpose flour
1 c	sugar	¼ t	salt
1 t	pure vanilla extract		

Directions: Mix butter and sugar by hand or in a mixer until just combined. Add the vanilla. Sift together the flour and the salt, then add them to the butter and sugar mixture until the dough just comes together. Dump onto a floured surface and gently shape into a disc and wrap in plastic to chill in the fridge for about a half hour.

Roll the dough about ½ inch thick and cut with a 2-inch round cutter. Place on an un-greased cutter sheet and bake for about 20 to 25 minutes until the edges are just beginning to brown. Cool to room temperature. If desired decorate with a cross motif with either a dusting of chocolate powder or melted chocolate chips drizzled atop.

Ark of the Covenant, pray for us!

Gate of Heaven, pray for us.

Our Lady of Lourdes
February 11

"And many that are first, shall be last: and the last shall be first."
—Matthew 19:30

Our Lady of Lourdes is celebrated on February 11 each year and is a significant feast that also impresses upon the faithful their love of Mary as the *Immaculate Conception*. We will attribute the symbolic title *Gate of Heaven* to Mary today from the *Litany of Loreto* because of Mary's "yes" to God and her undying devotion and love of all mankind and of us poor sinners.

Here is the story of Our Lady when she appeared to a small girl in a tiny village in France:

It was very cold on February 11, 1858, the day that was to mark the beginning of such an extraordinary series of events at the rock of Massabeille. When Bernadette returned from school her mother gave her permission to go down by the river to pick up driftwood and fallen branches. Toinette Marie, aged nine, and Marie Abadie, aged twelve, a neighbor's child, went with her. When the three girls reached the Massabeille, the two younger ones took off their wooden shoes to wade across an icy mill-stream which here joined the river. Bernadette, more sensitive, hung behind. Standing alone beside the river, she had started to remove her stockings when she heard a noise like a sudden rush of wind. Looking up towards the grotto she saw some movement among the branches, then there floated out of the opening a golden cloud, and in the midst of it was the figure of a beautiful young girl who placed herself in a small niche in the rock, at one side of the opening and slightly above it. In the crannies around this niche grew stunted vines and shrubs, and in particular a white eglantine. Bernadette, staring in fascination, saw that the luminous apparition was dressed in a soft white robe, with a broad girdle of blue, and a long white veil that partially covered her hair. Her eyes were blue and gentle. Golden roses gleamed on her bare feet. When the vision smiled and beckoned to Bernadette, the girl's fear vanished and she came a few steps nearer, then sank reverently to her knees. She drew her rosary from her pocket, for, in moments of stress, she habitually said her beads. The mysterious being also had a rosary, of large white beads, and to quote Bernadette's own account: "The Lady let me pray alone; she passed the beads of the rosary between her fingers, but said nothing; only at the end of each decade did she say the Gloria with me." When the recitation was finished, the Lady vanished into the cave and the golden mist disappeared with her. This experience affected Bernadette so powerfully that, when the other girls turned back to look for her, she was still kneeling, a rapt, faraway look on her face. They chided her, thinking she had passed the time praying to escape the task of gathering fuel. Tying up their twigs and branches into faggots, they started for home. Too full of her vision to keep quiet about it, before they had gone far Bernadette burst out with the whole wondrous story; she asked the girls to say nothing at home. But Toinette told Madame Soubirous that same evening, and soon the news spread further. Bernadette wished to go back to the Massabeille the next day, but her mother, after talking the matter over with a sister, refused her permission. On March 25, Lady Day, Bernadette started for the grotto at dawn. When the vision appeared to her, Bernadette said: *"Would you kindly tell me who you are?"* When the girl had repeated the question twice more, the Lady replied: *"I am the Immaculate Conception. I want a chapel here."* This answer, when reported by Bernadette, caused the local excitement to rise to a still higher pitch and the feeling grew that Bernadette's visitor was the Blessed Virgin. Only four years before the dogma of the Immaculate Conception had been promulgated. The seventeenth apparition took place on April 7, and the final one, more than three months later, on July 16. By that time, the grotto, which the people were trying to make into a sanctuary and place of worship, had been barricaded by the town authorities to discourage worshipers and curiosity-seekers from congregating there. During the twenty-one years that she was to remain on earth, Bernadette never again saw the vision. The accounts of what she had seen and heard, which she was obliged to repeat so often, never varied in any significant detail. —*Lives of Saints*, John J. Crawley & Co., Inc., 1954

It is hard for us to think of celebrating this lovely Feast without also thinking of the incredible faithfulness of Saint Bernadette. Her truly heartfelt and steadfast devotion to "Our Lady in the Grotto" is such a model of virtue for us, and so it is with our own children when we want them to learn about how special this title is of our Heavenly Queen. Bernadette was canonized in 1933. *"He has deposed the mighty from their thrones and raised the lowly to high places."* (Luke 1:52)

Teatime Chat

If you have decided to serve the *Tart Tatin* for your teatime today, explain that it is a French dessert and quite applicable to this feast. Talk about other favorite foods that might have originated in France: crepes, baguettes, croissants, escargot, steak au poivre, profiteroles! Have you ever had any of these foods with your family?

Devotional Activities

♥ *Our Lady of Lourdes Grotto*

Supplies: There is a fun to assemble pre-packaged grotto kit available (see resource Appendix D). If creating your own design, here are some suggested supplies needed: Small to medium shoebox or other suitable box or cardboard can be transformed into a grotto, holy card or picture of Our Lady and/or St. Bernadette, small polished rocks or flat blue marbles, different colors of craft paint, dried, silk or tissue paper flowers (real flowers can also be used in a tiny vase if desired), votive candle, tiny vase, aluminum foil.

Directions: Start with either a shoebox or other suitable box in whatever size you would like for your grotto. Cut off one square side and the flaps and used clear packing tape to make the shell of the Grotto. Paint the shell of the box inside and out a beautiful blue for Our Lady! Next paint clouds towards the top of the inside of the box, add cotton balls to create some dimension. Create the healing waters by cutting a small circle of aluminum foil and surround it with the flat blue marbles or stones on the inside bottom of the box. Add some flowers in the tiny vase next to the healing waters. You can use doubled pop-dots to install a holy card or alternatively just place your Marian statue inside the grotto and light your candle!

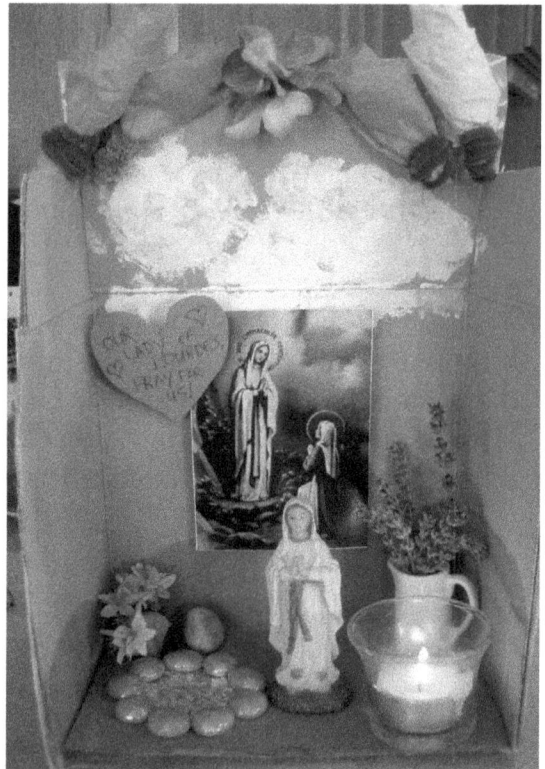

♥ **Read:** *Story of St. Bernadette*

♥ **Pray:** *Final Day of Novena to Our Lady of Lourdes*

♥ **Sing:** *Immaculate Mary*

♥ **Watch:** *Bernadette: Princess of Lourdes*, or *The Song of Bernadette*

Teatime Recipe Idea

Tart Tatin (Apple Crostata)

¼ t	kosher salt	1 ½ lbs	McIntosh, Gala or Empire Apples, peeled, cored and sliced or chunked
¼ t	cinnamon		
⊡ t	allspice	¼ t	grated orange or lemon zest
4 T	cold unsalted butter, diced	¼ c	all purpose flour
2 T	melted butter	¼ c	granulated or superfine sugar
		One Box Refrigerated Pie Crusts (2 in a box)	

Directions: Roll out each pastry into a large circle (about 11 inches). Make sure they do not tear. Place each pastry onto a cookie sheet or sheet lined with parchment. Brush lightly with melted butter.

For the filling: Toss sliced or chunked apples with the orange or lemon zest. Place apples onto the tart dough leaving about a 1½ inch border.

Combine the flour, sugar, salt, cinnamon, and allspice in the bowl. Cut in the butter until the mixture is crumbly. Sprinkle evenly over the apples. Gently fold the border over the apples, pleating it to make a circle.

Bake at 425°F for 20 to 25 minutes or until crust is golden brown and the apples are tender, but not mushy. Let cool on wire rack for 5 minutes, then serve sliced thick with ice cream, whip cream or a drizzle of Carmel sauce. Enjoy!

Gate of Heaven, pray for us!

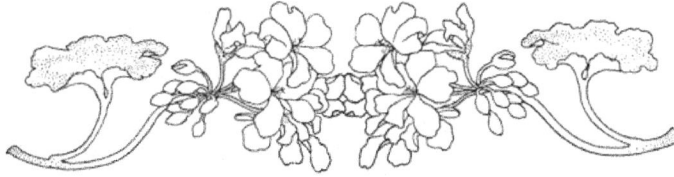

Morning Star, pray for us.

Our Lady, Star of the Sea
Moveable Feast

"Blessed are the eyes that see what you see!"
—Luke 10:23

Our Lady is the Morning Star and we celebrate her today as *Our Lady, Star of the Sea.* Mary being the Mother of God is truly the "light bearer" and what better symbolism to use for her in this title, than a Star, a beautiful, bright luminary leading us to her Son. A lighthouse is a beacon of light for sailors much like Mary is a beacon of the light of Christ. Seafarers worldwide invoke Mary in today's title to keep them safe at sea.

> *Mary means Star of the sea, for as mariners are guided to port by the ocean star, so Christians attain to glory through Mary's maternal intercession.*
> —St. Thomas Aquinas +1274

Christopher Columbus himself anchored his hopes of finding a new world with Our Lady at his side and nightly read the stars for guidance and hope of finding his destination. Mary is the guide on our heavenly path; fix your eyes on her as the luminous star that shows you the path to Jesus, the true "light bearer."

Teatime Chat

Here is a story about St. Bridget of Sweden that shows how the power of prayer and singing can be a devoted tribute to Our Lady and she will always keep you in her care:

It seems that during a riot in Rome, a mob came to the house where St. Bridget lived; a leader talked of burning Bridget alive. She prayed to Our Lord to know if she should flee to safety. Jesus advised her to stay: *"It does not matter if they plot Thy death. My power will break the malice of Thy enemies: if Mine crucified Me, it is because I permitted it."* Our Blessed Mother added: *"Sing as a group, the Ave Maris Stella and I'll guard you from every danger."* —*Pieta Prayer Booklet*, Miraculous Lady of Roses Corporation, 2006

Devotional Activities

♥ *Star of the Sea Paper Boxes*

Supplies: Gold or yellow scrapbook paper, shiny yellow or gold wrapping paper, pencil and a ruler.

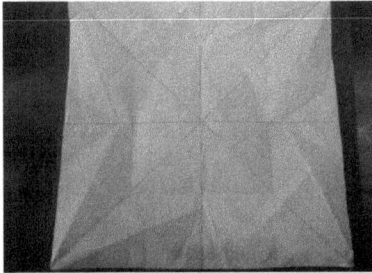

Directions:

1) To start with, lay a square of paper on the table in front of you and draw a line with your pencil from each point to point using a ruler as your guide.

2) Then again from side to side crossing in the center. You should have eight intersecting lines.

3) Now fold along these lines and crease, and then unfold them.

4) Now bring them together making sure to tuck the two sides in, it should be a diamond shape with two flaps in the middle.

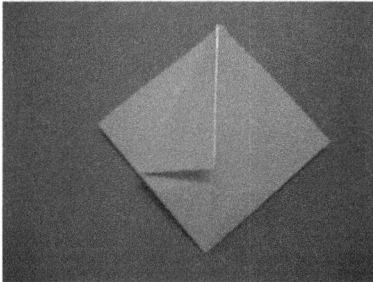

5) Making sure that the opening is at the top, fold one side along to the central fold and open up the small flap and press flat. Make sure these two folds line up. Tuck the left side of the small flap behind itself. Now repeat step (5) with the other side. Both sides should now look the same.

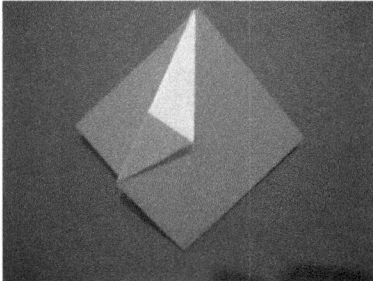

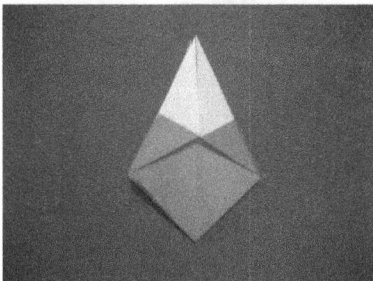

6) Turn it over so that the other side is showing. Do the same with the flaps at the back (step 5). The back should look exactly the same as the front.

7) Fold all four flaps down as far as they will go.

8) When you have folded two flaps down, pull the other two to the side and they will fold down too. Your box should start to open when you fold over the flaps.

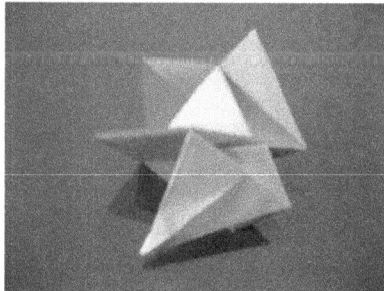

9) With your hand underneath, push up the middle and it will miraculously turn into a box. Neaten up the star flaps and fill with something special! This would make a lovely little rosary keeper to give and to receive!

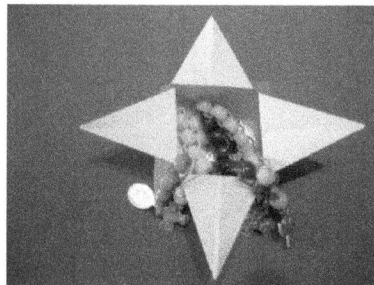

110

♥ *Seashore Altar decorations*

Collect various shells and create a beautiful nature scene on your altar for Mary. Sand filled votives would be a lovely addition and represent Mary well as "light bearer."

♥ **Sing or pray:** *Ave Maris Stella*

♥ **Poetry:** *Star of the Sea* (included below)

Star of the Sea

When evening shades are falling
O'er ocean's sunny sleep,
To pilgrims' hearts recalling
Their home beyond the deep;

When rest, o'er all descending,
The shores with gladness smile,
And lutes, their echoes blending,
Are heard from isle to isle:

Then Mary, Star of the Sea,
We pray, we pray, to thee.
The noon-day tempest over,
Now ocean toils no more,

And wings of halcyons hover,
Where all was strife before.
Oh thus may life, in closing,
It's short tempestuous day,

Beneath heaven's smile reposing,
Shine all its storms away:
Thus, Mary Star of the Sea,
We pray, we pray, to thee!

—Thomas Moore, 1844

Teatime Recipe Idea

Star Anise Cookies

2 T	star anise pieces		2 T	balsamic vinegar
½ c	sugar		¼ c	all purpose flour
5 T	unsalted butter			

Directions: Preheat oven to 350°F and line 2 large baking sheets with parchment paper. In a sturdy mortar and pestle, grind the whole star anise pods until fine. Alternately you can use an electric coffee/spice grinder to finely grind star anise. In a 1 to 1 ½ quart heavy saucepan bring anise, sugar, butter, and vinegar to a boil over moderate heat, stirring, and boil 1 minute. Remove pan from heat and stir in flour and a pinch salt until mixture is smooth. Cool dough to room temperature.

Form and bake cookies as directed at below: Roll level ½ t dough into balls and arrange 4 inches apart on baking sheets. Bake cookies in batches in upper and lower thirds of oven, switching position of sheets halfway through baking, 10 minutes, or until cookies are flat and golden. Transfer parchment with cookies to racks to cool. Cool baking sheets and line with fresh parchment between batches.

Star of the Sea, pray for us!

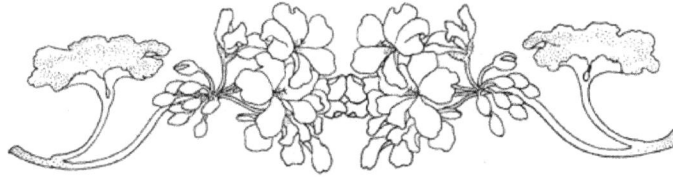

Health of the Sick, pray for us.

Our Lady of Perpetual Help
June 27

"Let hearts rejoice who search for the Lord. Seek the Lord and his strength; seek always the face of the Lord."—Psalm 104:3-4

To think of something as perpetual, it is ongoing, never-ending, for always. This is what devotion to Our Lady is. Her love, like that of God's is unconditional, perpetual and so full of goodness and mercy, it can never be extinguished, not even after death.

As *Health of the Sick* we can look to Mary as our guide through life. This beautiful invocation expresses Our Lady's invariable mercy in perpetuity towards us. It is an act of uninterrupted piety, assistance and grace, and it is there every time we call on her holy name. Devotion to Our Lady in this title was spread throughout the Church by the Redemptorist priests and the faithful call on Mary for her perpetual and divine goodness in this title, *Our Lady of Perpetual Help.*

Teatime Chat

Today is a good day to talk about elderly people, or those who are home bound for one reason or another. Grandparents may fit into this category. If you cannot go for a visit, a phone call or special letter sent today in their honor would be delightful.

Be a friend to the elderly. They might seem frail and graying, even though they were once young like you. It is important to show the proper love and respect to a grandparent or older person. Although they may be grouchy towards us, they still need our love. When you are visiting, offer to help out all you can.

113

Rise in the presence of the aged, show respect for the elderly
and revere your God. —(Leviticus 19:32)

Ask for the grace of *Our Lady of Perpetual Help* in all that you seek for the Kingdom of God. As a model of contemplation, she is our help, our sweetness and our life!

Devotional Activities

♥ *Health of the Sick Feel Better Bags*

Supplies: small sacks, either purchased gift bags or hand-sown fabric bags filled with essential "feel good" necessities. Some suggestions might be: a spiritual bouquet (refer to the *Visitation* entry), holy cards or medals, band-aids, hand or foot cream, calling card, tea bag or hot cocoa mix, lavender filled sachets, bubble bath beads, small scented candle, suntan lotion, deck of cards, and on, and on....Have fun thinking of more goodies to include ☺

♥ *Offer a Mass for someone who is aging or elderly*

♥ *Visit someone who is home bound*

♥ *Study the symbolism* in the icon of *Our Lady of Perpetual Help*. You can find a holy card of the image at any Catholic gift store, or view the image online (http://www.our-lady.net/our-lady-of-perpetual-help.php). The icon represents the archangels showing the child Jesus the instruments of His passion with the child Jesus taking refuge in Our Lady's arms. Greek initials at the top represent "Mother of God." Those near the angels represent their names and the those the right of Christ represent "Jesus Christ."

Golden Crown: placed on the original picture by order of the Holy See in 1867. It is a token of the many miracles wrought by Our Lady invoked under the title of "Perpetual Help."

Star on Our Lady's Veil: symbolizes Mary as Star of the Sea who brought the light of Christ to the darkened world, the light that brings us to Heaven.

St Gabriel, the Archangel *(right side):* holds the cross and nails.

St Michael, the Archangel (left side): holds the lance and gall-sop of Christ's passion.

Mary's Eyes: large for all our trouble, turned toward us, not baby Jesus.

Mary's Mouth: small to represent her silent recollection.

Red Tunic: the color worn by virgins at the time of Christ.

Dark Blue Mantle: the color worn by mothers in Palestine. Her garments show her to be both virgin and mother

Christ's Hands: turned palms down into His mother's indicate that the graces of redemption are in her keeping.

Mary's Left Hand: supporting Christ possessively as she is His mother. It is a comforting hand for everyone who calls on her.

Foot with Falling Sandal: symbolizes Christ's Divine nature, barely clinging to the earth. His human nature is symbolized in the other foot to which the sandal is more firmly bound. Christ's two natures—human and divine—in one Divine Person. (Source: Redemptorist Fathers, St. Alphonsus Parish)

Prayer to Our Lady of Perpetual Help

> *O Mother of Perpetual Help, grant that I may ever invoke thy most powerful name, which is the safeguard of the living and the salvation of the dying. O Purest Mary, O Sweetest Mary, let thy name henceforth be ever on my lips. Delay not, O Blessed Lady, to help me whenever I call on thee, for, in all my needs, in all my temptations I shall never cease to call on thee, ever repeating thy sacred name, Mary, Mary.*
>
> *O what consolation, what sweetness, what confidence, what emotion fill my soul when I pronounce thy sacred name, or even only think of thee. I thank God for having given thee, for my good, so sweet, so powerful, so lovely a name. But I will not be content with merely pronouncing thy name: let my love for thee prompt me ever to hail thee, Mother of Perpetual Help.*

Teatime Recipe Idea

Chamomile Tea served with honey.

It might also be a fun day to pull out those cans of *Chicken Noodle soup* (you know the red and white labeled ones in the back of the pantry). Enjoy some American soup while you think about those in need of some healing today!

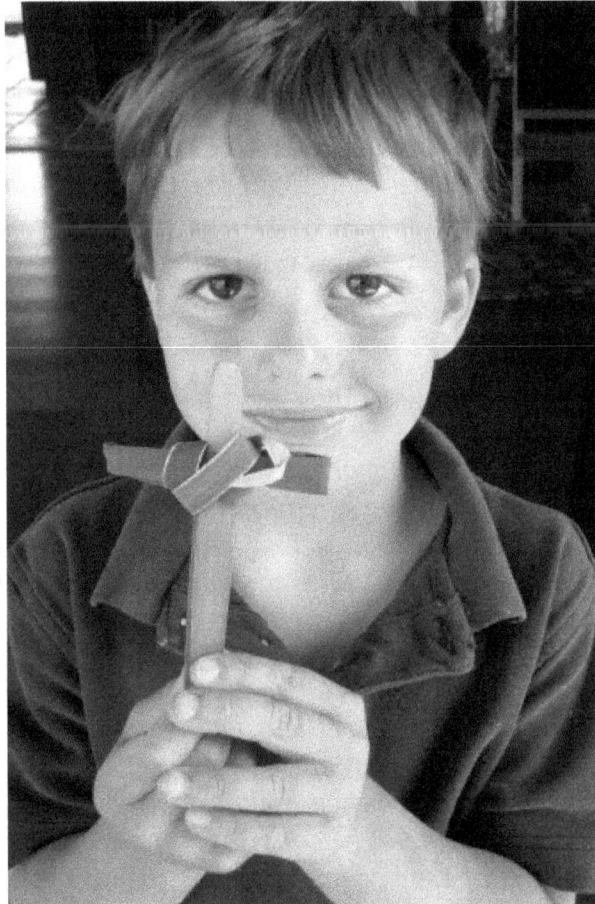

Health of the Sick, pray for us!

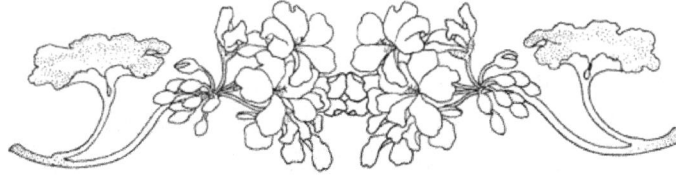

Refuge of Sinners, pray for us.

Our Lady, Refuge of Sinners
August 13

"You will remember me as sweeter than honey, better to have than the honeycomb." —Sirach 24: 19

Our Blessed Mother is often referred to as *Refuge of Sinners.* As our heavenly Mother, she has compassion for the misery of poor sinners. As we honor Mary today in this symbolic title you will learn the *Memorare.* It is interesting to note that this anonymous prayer originated in the 15th century and it is sometimes attributed to such famous saints as Augustine, John Chrysostom, and Bernard of Clairvaux. *Memorare* is Latin for "remember." Have your children listen carefully today as you pray the *Litany of Loreto.* It will be fun to see if they can hear when this title comes. You will also learn about a special herb attributed to Our Lady and enjoy some of its deliciousness if you are having teatime.

Remember, O most gracious Virgin Mary, that never was it known that anyone who fled to your protection, implored your help, or sought your intercession was left unaided. Inspired by this confidence, I fly unto you, O Virgin of virgins, my Mother. To you I come, before you I stand, sinful and sorrowful. O Mother of the Word Incarnate, despise not my petitions, but in your mercy hear and answer me. Amen.

Teatime Chat

Your children will like hearing about how we can go to Mary when we sin and ask for her help in petitioning Jesus for His mercy towards us. When we go "*to Jesus, through Mary*" she becomes our *refuge* and her intercession on our behalf will have an everlasting effect on Our Lord in forgiving our sins. *"God is our refuge and our strength, an ever-present help in our distress."* (Psalm 46:1)

Explain how herbs like Rosemary were created by God to aid our memory. Honey in our tea reminds us of Mary, that she is our sweetness and our hope! Rosemary is also an herb typically served with lamb dishes and Eastertime specialty.

Devotional Activities

♥ *Memorare Bookmarks*

Supplies: Strips of colored cardstock, gold or silver ribbon, holy cards of Mary, stickers, fun brads or buttons, printed copies of the *Memorare* prayer printed and sized to fit bookmarks, or the prayer can be handwritten as well.

Directions: Cut cardstock into desired strips (usually 2" × 6") for bookmarks, then have each child attach their prayer first, the Holy card of Mary next, and then decorate as desired with ribbons, stickers, etc. Display on your Mary altar today and save for gifts or use immediately in one of your favorite books!

♥ *Rosemary Terracotta Pots*

Supplies: Rosemary starts, terracotta pots about 3-5 inches, craft paint (optional).

Directions: Plant small Rosemary starts in three or four inch terra cotta pots. If you want to make them extra fancy, you could paint the pots with some symbols of Mary: A crescent moon, eight-pointed star, Mary's Immaculate Heart encircled by roses, the capital letter "M" with a cross rising from it's center. As you plant your mini-trees, talk about how Rosemary is good for remembrance.

As for Rosmarine, I let it run all over my garden walls, not only because my bees love it, but because it is the herb sacred to remembrance, and, therefore, to friendship; whence a sprig of it hath a dumb language that makes it the chosen emblem of our funeral wakes and in our burial grounds. —Sir Thomas More d. 1535

Teatime Recipe Idea

Morning Biscuits with Rosemary

1½ c	unbleached flour		1 T	sugar
½ c	whole wheat flour		¾ c	milk
1 t	baking powder		2 T	butter
½ t	baking soda		2 t	crumbled, dried rosemary
dash	salt			(or 2 T fresh, chopped)

Excluding the rosemary, sift dry ingredients together in a large bowl. With a fork or pastry cutter, work the butter into the dry ingredients, some small lumps will remain. Add the rosemary and milk and mix well to form a soft dough.

Roll out the dough to ½ inch thickness on a lightly floured surface. Cut into 2 inch rounds and place on a greased and lightly floured baking sheet. Bake for 20 minutes at 400°F. Makes about 1½ dozen.

Serve with Rosemary Tea sweetened with honey.

Our Lady, Refuge of Sinners, pray for us!

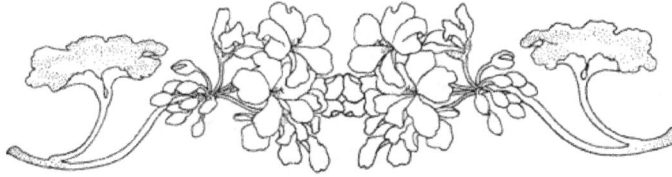

Comforter of the Afflicted, pray for us.

Our Lady of Sorrows
September 15

"But she said to them, "Do not call me Naomi. Call me Mara, for the Almighty has made it very bitter for me." —Ruth 1:20

At the Presentation of Jesus in the temple, Mary received prophetic news from the aging Simeon that her son would be "a light to lighten the Gentiles, and the glory of the people Israel..." (Luke 2:32) He also said that because of this prophecy and revelation that "thy own soul, a sword shall pierce . . . " (Luke 2:35)

How could Mary know that in her innocence, goodness and purity she would also be a witness to the ultimate Passion and death of her beloved son? Saint Joseph had long since passed into his eternal glory, and Mary who "pondered and kept everything in her heart" (Luke 2: 19) at Jesus' birth would bear this painful set of events at the end of Jesus' earthly life alone. How utterly sorrowful and painful it must have been to walk that road to Calvary with Jesus, knowing what would come to pass.

This feast of Our Lady of Sorrows shows Mary as *Comforter of the Afflicted.* We usually go to Mary in our joy and gladness, so this particular devotion to Mary may seem a little sad, especially for young children but we need not approach it in a depressing way. Today we are going to make a beautiful garden representing the Seven Sorrows of Mary and thus bring joy to her and Jesus on their heavenly thrones.

Teatime Chat

Please do not feel like you have to re-visit all of your Holy Week activities and the full Passion play, but rather make it a time to look briefly at each of the seven sorrows of Mary's life and in turn create something special with symbolic flowers for Mary. The tradition of creating a garden devoted to Our Lady dates back to medieval times. I have also provided an example of a container garden that my dear children and I have created for this feast. I hope you will use it as a springboard to launch your own inspiration.

Seven Sorrows of Mary

Prophecy of Simeon (Luke 2:34-35)
Flight into Egypt (Matthew 2:13-15)
Jesus lost in the temple (Luke 2:45-51)
Jesus meets his afflicted mother (Luke 23:27-31)
Jesus is crucified (John 19:25-27)
Jesus is taken down from the cross (Luke 23:50-56)
Jesus is laid in the tomb (Mark 15:46-47)

Devotional Activities

♥ **Display: *Michelangelo's Pieta*** (can be found doing an online search and printed out on photo quality paper)

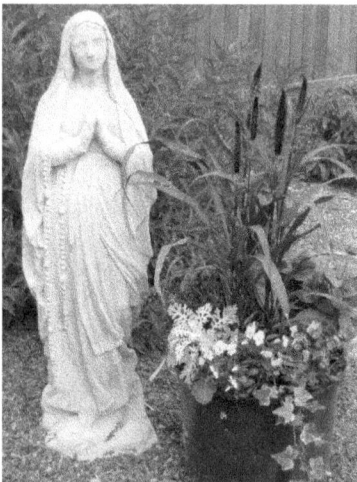

♥ *Gardens or Mini-gardens*

Supplies: If you are going to do mini-gardens for each child, then make sure you have all the necessary pots, plants, potting soil and large spoons or shovels ready for easy assembly come activity time. 7" – 9" inch terra-cotta pots would be lovely, or you have the option of adding to an already planted Mary Garden out of doors. A large container garden is great too.

♥ **Flowers to consider for your Mary garden**

>Iris (Sword of sorrow)
>Lily of the Valley, Larkspur (Mary's tears)
>Maidenhair Fern (Mary's tresses)
>Toadflax (Mary's torn tresses)
>English Daisy (Mother of God's flower)
>Morning Glory (Lady's mantle)
>Sweet Alyssum (Mary's little cross)
>Forget-me-Nots (Eyes of Mary)
>Petunia (Our Lady's praises)
>Roses (Mary)

If you are doing a larger plotted garden, consider placing a statue of Our Lady somewhere among the flowers, she will be very happy there! Here are some flowers we chose one year for our container garden.

Mary's Sword (Iris): since irises were unavailable, we used grasses to remind us of Simeon's prophetic message to Mary, "that a sword will pierce her heart . . ."

Ivy (*Hedera helix*): for Mary's everlasting and constant love of Jesus.

Dusty Miller (*Senecio cineraria*): the grey velvety foliage of this plant symbolizes the silver moonlight under which Our Lady and her newborn babe must have traveled during their flight into Egypt.

Gloriosa Daisy (*Rudbeckia tetra gloriosa*): the Gloriosa Daisy which is St. Anthony's flower represents taking down Jesus' body from the cross.

Pansy (*Viola tricolor*): we chose these in blue (*Sorbet Beaconsfield*) to tie in with Mary's Mantle and white (*Sorbet Coconut*) to represent God's heavenly light that shines perpetually on Mary in her goodness even at the crucifixion.

Chrysanthemum (*Chrysanthemum indicum*): this is known as the All Saints flower and while not specifically representative of her sorrow, we want to acknowledge that Mary triumphs and is eventually crowned Queen of All the Saints.

♥ Pray or Sing: *Stabat Mater Dolorosa*

♥ Pray: *Litany of the Seven Sorrows of Mary* Composed by Pope Pius VII while held in captivity by Napoleon. (For private devotion only)

V. Lord, have mercy on us.
R. Christ, have mercy on us.

V. Lord, have mercy on us. Christ, hear us.
R. Christ, graciously hear us.

God, the Father of heaven,
have mercy on us.
God the Son, Redeemer of the world,
have mercy on us.
God the Holy Spirit, have mercy on us.

Holy Mary, Mother of God, pray for us.
Holy Virgin of virgins, pray for us.
Mother of the Crucified, [etc.]
Sorrowful Mother
Mournful Mother
Sighing Mother
Afflicted Mother
Forsaken Mother
Desolate Mother
Mother most sad
Mother set around with anguish
Mother overwhelmed by grief
Mother transfixed by a sword
Mother crucified in thy heart
Mother bereaved of thy Son
Sighing Dove
Mother of Dolors
Fount of tears
Sea of bitterness
Field of tribulation
Mass of suffering

Mirror of patience
Rock of constancy
Remedy in perplexity
Joy of the afflicted
Ark of the desolate
Refuge of the abandoned
Shield of the oppressed
Conqueror of the incredulous
Solace of the wretched
Medicine of the sick
Help of the faint
Strength of the weak
Protectress of those who fight
Haven of the shipwrecked
Calmer of tempests
Companion of the sorrowful

Retreat of those who groan
Terror of the treacherous
Standard-bearer of the Martyrs
Treasure of the Faithful
Light of Confessors
Pearl of Virgins
Comfort of Widows
Joy of all Saints
Queen of thy Servants
Holy Mary, who alone art unexampled

V. Pray for us, most Sorrowful Virgin,
R. That we may be made worthy of the
promises of Christ.

Let us pray: O God, in whose Passion, according to the prophecy of Simeon, a sword of grief pierced through the most sweet soul of Thy glorious Blessed Virgin Mother Mary: grant that we, who celebrate the memory of her Seven Sorrows, may obtain the happy effect of Thy Passion, Who lives and reigns world without end. Amen.

You have created lovely and heartfelt devotion to Mary in her sorrows today, and you have also introduced to your children a way to love Mary when she is at her saddest time. She remained at the foot of the cross, and your garden will remind you and your children that we will also share in her sorrowing and be blessed by her strength, beauty and presence.

Teatime Recipe Idea Luncheon

Seven Herb Soup

*Special Note – Today rather than a sweet treat for teatime, I am recommending a special *"Seven Herb Soup"* as a luncheon that is traditionally served during Lent, but is totally appropriate for a Marian Feast.

2 c	potatoes, peeled and diced	spinach, chicory, green onions, collards, kale, mustard and turnip greens,
2 c	leeks, washed, sliced	
½ c	heavy cream	
2	quarts chicken broth	Salt
1 to 2 c	mixed chopped greens	White pepper to taste
watercress, broccoli, broccolini, broccoli rabe, beet greens, or dandelion greens		1 lemon juiced
		Parsley chopped for garnish

Directions: Place the potatoes, leeks and broth in a large saucepan. Add 1 t salt and bring to a boil. Simmer, partly covered for about 20 minutes or until the potatoes and leeks are tender. Add the greens and simmer for 5 to 10 minutes longer, or until the greens have just become tender.

Puree the mixture in a blender or food processor, adding the heavy cream as you blend.

Pour the soup into a serving bowl or tureen. Add the white pepper to taste and the lemon juice. Taste for seasoning. If you plan to serve the soup cold, over salt it slightly. If the soup seems too thick, add a little chicken broth or if it's too thin, add some more heavy cream. Chill for several hours. I love this soup hot too and for this luncheon, it will be ready in no time! Serve with thick sliced French bread or rolls.

*Also note that if you want to stick to a teatime event, then you can simply have:
Black or Herbal Tea – no milk or sugar, or alternatively choose water

Cross Cookies (or no treat as a sacrifice)

Comforter of the Afflicted, pray for us!

Iris, Our Lady's Sword

126

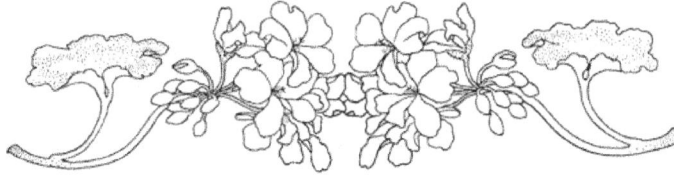

Help of Christians, pray for us.

Our Lady, Help of Christians
May 24

"I will put enmities between thee and the woman, and thy seed and her seed: she shall crush thy head, and thou shalt lie in wait for her heel."

—Genesis 3:15

In celebration of Our Lady, Help of Christians today we honor Mary with a grateful heart. God chose her to be our mediator in our struggle for heaven and for this, we rejoice.

Catholics have called upon Mary in times of adversity, strife, persecutions, and war for thousands of years. She is the vanquisher of evil, and we need her protection. After a naval battle was won at Lepanto by invoking Our Lady, Pope Pius V inserted the title "Help of Christians" into the *Litany of Loreto*. When everything seemed lost, Mary interceded to help the Christians defeat the invading Muslim Turks. The prayers of the faithful showed true fidelity to Our Lady, a confidence that the fate of Christendom was in her loving hands and that she would give victory to the soldiers that day. Mary's help gives all souls a hope to win the battle for the greater glory of God.

Later, Pius the VII instituted the feast of *Our Lady, Help of Christians* after he was unexpectedly released early from prison under the rule of Napoleon I.

Because Mary is the bearer of joy, she readies all Christians to receive God's grace and the many gifts of life. Mary again crushes the head of the serpent with her heel and we as God's people triumph.

What Lucifer lost by pride Mary won by humility. What Eve ruined and lost by disobedience Mary saved by obedience. By obeying the serpent, Eve ruined her children as well as herself and delivered them up to him. Mary by her perfect fidelity to God saved her children with herself and consecrated them to his divine majesty.

— *True Devotion*, no. 53, Saint Louis de Montfort

Teatime Chat

Mary is a beacon of hope in our fallen world of today. She is a glimmer of the light of Christ. Just as Mary crushes the head of the serpent and keeps the devil at bay, we too can be crusaders like Mary and that of *Help of Christians* in all that we say and do. We can be a glimmer of hope for others as we live out the gospel of Christ.

Make a list with your children today of all the different ways you and your family can be crusaders for Christ. Start with praying the rosary as a family if this is not already a family practice!

Put on the armor of God, that you may be able to stand against the deceits of the devil. For our wrestling is not against flesh and blood; but against principalities and power, against the rulers of the world of this darkness, against the spirits of wickedness in the high places. Therefore take unto you the armor of God, that you may be able to resist in the evil day, and to stand in all things perfect. Stand therefore, having your loins girt about with truth, and having on the breastplate of justice, And your feet shod with the preparation of the gospel of peace: In all things taking the shield of faith, wherewith you may be able to extinguish all the fiery darts of the most wicked one. And take unto you the helmet of salvation, and the sword of the Spirit (which is the word of God).
                                                              — Ephesians 6:11-17

Devotional Activities

♥ *Shields or Standards for Our Lady*

Supplies: Pieces of cardboard or cereal boxes, aluminum foil, fabric, stickers, markers, packing or duct tape, pipe cleaners, glue stick, scissors.

Directions: Cut shields out of cardboard or a cereal box about 9 × 15 inches and cover with aluminum foil, making sure to secure on the backside of the shield with some of the packing or duct tape. Decorate with fabric, use markers to draw Marian symbols, cover with stickers, or simply have your children draw a design of their own. These will be a sign of bravery and preparation for battle, which we need to arm ourselves against the devil on a daily basis. Taping a sturdy cord or the pipe cleaner for a handgrip on the back middle of the shield works well for outdoor play!

♥ Pray: *Prayer to Mary, Help of Christians*

> *Mary, powerful Virgin, you are the mighty and glorious protector of the Church. You are the marvelous help of Christians. You are awe-inspiring as an army in battle array. You eliminated heresy in the world. Amid our anguish, struggle, and distress, defend us from the power of the enemy, and at the hour of our death receive our soul in heaven.*
>
> —St. John Bosco, d. 1888

Teatime Recipe Idea

Deviled Worms

Serve gummy worms immersed in flavored gelatin to emphasize Mary crushing the head of the serpent. Juice would work well today! Alternatively, your favorite recipe for Deviled Eggs served with a spear and an olive might be a nice touch. Here's one we like:

Deviled Eggs

1-2 dozen	hard-boiled eggs	½ - 1 c	mayonnaise
1 ½ t	salt	2-3 T	Dijon-style mustard
1 t	freshly cracked pepper		Paprika for garnish, black olives

Directions: Peel hard-boiled eggs and slice in two. Remove yolks and place in a bowl. Add all ingredients except garnishes and combine until smooth. A fork works well for this. Scoop yolk mixture into halved whites, dust with paprika and place a speared olive through the top of each.

Help of Christians, pray for us!

Part 4

Mary, Our Queen

MARY QUEEN OF HEAVEN AND EARTH

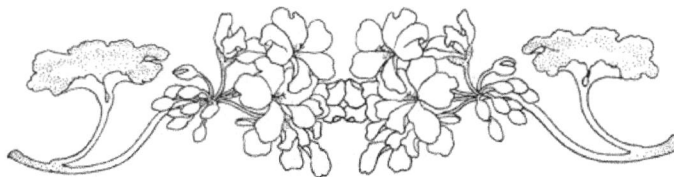

Queen of Angels, Patriarchs, Prophets, Apostles, Martyrs, Confessors, Virgins, All Saints, pray for us.

Queen-ship of Mary
August 22

"And thou shalt be a crown of glory in the hand of the Lord, and a royal diadem in the hand of thy God." —Isaiah 62:3

Mary is crowned as Queen of all heaven and earth and as we recite the glorious titles in the *Litany of Loreto* today, we are reminded of her place in God's heavenly house. She is above all our Queen and our Mother. As a beautiful reflection of God's love for His people, she points not to her own glory, but to His. She has been enthroned by God for life everlasting with Him who is glory and praise forever!

"The queen stands at your right hand arrayed in cloth of gold."
—(Psalm 44:10)

Our feast today follows the *Solemnity of the Assumption of Mary* by exactly one week or on its "octave" which is fitting in that she has just been assumed into heaven and is now seated next to her king. *"The hand of the Lord was upon me, and brought me forth in the spirit of the Lord: and set me down in the midst of a plain."* (Ezekiel 37:1)

Teatime Chat

The *Salve Regina*, or *Hail Holy Queen*, is the most popular prayer to Mary after the Angelical Salutation (Hail Mary) of Saint Gabriel the Archangel. It is said after Mass, after compline and at the conclusion of the

Holy Rosary. Singing this beautiful prayer is our most favorite way of celebrating Mary at the conclusion of our daily rosary.

Here is the prayer as written by Blessed Herman the Cripple and then finished by St. Bernard (d. 1153):

> *Hail, holy Queen, Mother of mercy, our life, our sweetness and our hope. To thee do we cry, poor banished children of Eve: to thee do we send up our sighs, mourning and weeping in this valley of tears. Turn then O most gracious advocate, Thine eyes of mercy toward us, and after this our exile, show unto us the blessed fruit of thy womb, Jesus, O clement, O loving, O sweet Virgin Mary! Pray for us O Holy Mother of God, that we may be made worthy of the promises of Christ.*

Devotional Activities

♥ *Crowns for Mary*

Supplies: Construction paper, felt or stiff fabric, or a pre-purchased crown from a party or paper crafts store.

Directions: Decorate pre-made crowns or cut out your own then add jewels, stickers, paint or whatever you may have on hand. Let everyone enjoy wearing their crowns at teatime, or for a special dinnertime celebration with the whole family blessing Mary as Queen of Heaven and Earth!

♥ Sing: *Hail Holy Queen Enthroned Above* or *Salve Regina*

♥ Pray: *5th Glorious Mystery of the rosary* Coronation of the Blessed Virgin Mary

> *Rise up in splendor! Your light has come, the glory of the Lord shines upon you. See, darkness covers the earth, and thick clouds cover the peoples; But upon you the Lord shines, and over you appears his glory. Nations shall walk by your light and kings by your shining radiance. Raise your eyes and look about; they all gather and come to you: Your sons come from afar, and your daughters in the arms of their nurses.*
>
> —Psalm 60:1-4

Teatime Recipe Idea

Crown Cake or Cupcakes

Decorate as desired to represent Mary's crown as she sits on her heavenly throne with Jesus!

Queen of Angels, Patriarchs, Prophets, Apostles, Martyrs, Confessors, Virgins, All Saints, pray for us!

Roses, Symbol of the Queenship of Mary

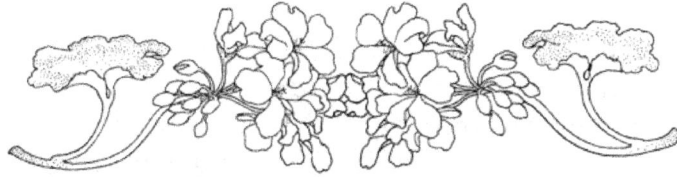

Queen Conceived Without Original Sin, pray for us.

Solemnity of the Immaculate Conception
of the Blessed Virgin Mary
December 8

The Blessed Virgin Mary in the first instance of her conception, by a singular privilege and grace granted by God, in view of the merits of Jesus Christ, the Savior of the human race, was preserved exempt from all stain of original sin. —Pius IX Ineffabilis Deus

Today's feast of the Blessed Virgin Mary's Immaculate Conception is the most solemn of all feasts in which the church celebrates during this holy time of Advent. As we honor Our Blessed Mother as Queen Conceived Without Original Sin we are reminded of the fall of man at the moment that Adam and Eve consumed the apple from the Forbidden Tree. God's plan to preserve Mary from original sin is miraculous and mysterious at the same time. Her Immaculate Conception is truly one of the mysteries of the church, but like any good mystery, it is meant to be contemplated and meditated upon with great interest and pondering.

The "splendor of an entirely unique holiness" by which Mary is "enriched from the first instant of her conception" comes wholly from Christ: she is "redeemed, in a more exalted fashion, by reason of the merits of her Son." The Father blessed Mary more than any other created person "in Christ with every spiritual blessing in the heavenly places" and chose her "in Christ before the foundation of the world, to be holy and blameless before him in love." —CCC 492, Ephesians 1:3-4

137

We have been given new light on a truth that the Church has universally honored since its declaration by Pope Pius IX in 1854. To celebrate this solemnity of the *Immaculate Conception of Mary* is a joyful anticipation that reminds us that the Birth of Jesus is not far off. Mary is truly "full of grace" and we acknowledge her today as Queen and conqueror of all!

Teatime Chat

Mother's Day in December? Why not? According to Meredith Gould, in *The Catholic Home* (Random House, New York, 2004) it is a Spanish custom to celebrate mothers and motherhood on this day. During your *Immaculate Tea*, have the children shower you (or your own mother or mother-in-law) with special cards and lots of hugs, you will (they will) especially appreciate them at this extra busy time of year!

Devotional Activities

♥ *Mother's Day Cards*

Supplies: Have your usual supply of stickers, stamps and cardstock available for the creativity to abound!

Directions: Create special mother's day cards for all the mothers, and grandmothers in your life and present them today!

♥ *Pure White Pillar Candle*

Supplies: One tall 3-inch wide white pillar candle, white silk roses, white ribbon, white glitter pens, glue stick.

Decorate as desired, let dry and light at your Immaculate Tea!

♥ *Attend Mass* (Holy Day of Obligation)

♥Sing: *Immaculate Mary*

♥ **Pray:** *O God who by the Immaculate Conception of the Blessed Virgin Mary, have prepared a worthy dwelling place for your Son, we humbly beg of you, that through the death of your Son, which you foreknew, You have kept her free from all sin, so by her intercession enable us also to come to You, with pure hearts. We ask this through the same Christ our Lord. Amen.* —Collect for the Feast of the Immaculate Conception

Teatime Recipe Idea

Immaculate Tea for Mother's Day in December

Use your imagination with this idea as you are representing Mary's immaculate and perfect purity. You could have a "pure" white selection of tea treats such as: a white cake or cupcakes decorated with white roses (real or artificial), white bread tea sandwiches with cream cheese, clam chowder, vanilla ice cream, pure vanilla milk tea, good old cold milk. The possibilities are endless.

Decorate your teatime table with all white table linens today or other white table decorations.

White hot chocolate would be a special treat today and would represent well Mary's purity.

White Hot Chocolate *(serves 8 to 10) Makes 9 cups.*

4 c	whole milk		1 lb.	white chocolate, chopped
4 c	half-and-half		2 t	vanilla extract

Directions: In a medium saucepan, heat the milk and half-and-half to just below the simmering point. Remove the pan from the heat and add the white chocolate. When the chocolate is melted, add the vanilla and whisk to blend. Reheat gently and serve.

Queen Conceived without original sin, pray for us!

Carnation for the Assumption

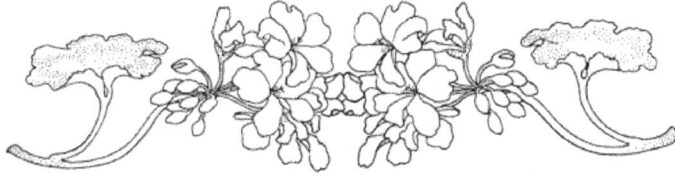

Queen Assumed into Heaven, pray for us.

Solemnity of the Assumption of the Blessed Virgin Mary
August 15

In giving birth you kept your virginity; in your Dormition you did not leave the world, O Mother Of God, but were joined to the source of life. You conceived the living God and, by your prayers, will deliver our souls from death.

—Byzantine Liturgy, Troparian, Feast of the Dormition, August 15

Our dearest Mary was exempt from the fires of eternal sin and by her obedience she helped to save all of mankind as well. It is right that she should be assumed body and soul into God's heavenly kingdom to sit with her Son in eternal glory.

We celebrate this title of Mary in the *Litany of Loreto* as *Queen Assumed into Heaven*. By the grace of God, she is truly a temple of the Holy Spirit and the divine word become flesh. As Queen of Heaven and earth, she bestows upon us lowly servants some of God's grace from the throne. Through the Apostles and Saints, we revere her eternal glory forever!

Teatime Chat

August is an incredible time of abundance in the garden. If you are so lucky to enjoy roses from your garden these will represent well Our Lady on her Assumption day. If not roses, white lilies if you can find them. The carnation can also be substituted for the roses. Some of the great artists of the Renaissance depicted Our Lady with carnations in and amongst the roses and lilies in their renditions of the Assumption, and no matter what flower is chosen, she is always our Queen of all God's creations. Bartolomeo Della Gatta's *Assumption* from the 15th century depicts beautifully Mary's tomb filled with flowers. It might be nice to locate some of his beautiful artwork online to show your children today while you are celebrating this feast of Mary.

The Italians have a special custom of delivering fruit baskets and feasting on all fruit for today! Enjoy a fruit salad with your dinner and display your beautiful Marzipan fruit creations as a centerpiece around Our Lady! If you are having the Blackberry Tarts at teatime, might I suggest that you drizzle them in vanilla flavored heavy cream and you too can assume yourself into heaven!

Devotional Activities (choose one or more)

♥ *Marzipan Fruit Baskets*

Supplies: Marzipan (found in the baking isle at your local grocers), assorted food colors, toothpicks, small baskets or gift bags. Decorating supplies can also be acquired at the craft store in the cake-decorating aisle.

Directions: Have fun creating delicate little marzipan fruit delights to put into tiny baskets from the craft store. Since this is an Italian custom of delivering fruit baskets on this day, why not include some yummy biscotti or a box of chocolate covered espresso beans, yum (not for the little ones however, do take care)!

♥ *Attend Mass* (Holy day of obligation)

♥ Deliver: *Fresh fruit baskets* (as an alternative to the marzipan)

♥ Pray:

> *All-powerful and ever-living God, you raised the sinless Virgin Mary, mother of your Son, body and soul to the glory of heaven. May we see heaven as our final goal and come to share her glory. We ask this through our Lord Jesus Christ, your Son, who lives and reigns with you and the Holy Spirit one God, forever and ever.* —Opening prayer, Solemnity of the Assumption of the Blessed Virgin Mary

Teatime Recipe Idea

Blackberry Tarts *(or a combination of summer berries of your choice)*

For the Tart Shells: (You can buy these pre-made if you prefer)

2 c	all purpose flour		½ c	unsalted butter, chilled
1 t	salt		3 T	margarine, chilled
			6 T	ice water

Directions: To make the tart shells, sift the flour and salt together into a bowl. Cut the butter and margarine into ½ inch chunks and add them to the flour mixture. Blend with a pastry blender until pea-sized balls form. Add the ice water 1 T at a time. After each addition of water, turn with a fork and then your fingertips. This will help to keep the pastry light and flaky. Try not to overwork the dough or it will become tough. Gather the dough into a ball and wrap in plastic wrap to chill for about 15 minutes.

Preheat the oven to 350°F. On a lightly floured work surface, roll out the dough to ⬚ of an inch thick. Lift dough into the tart pan(s) and press gently to shape it into the pan. You can mold the edges with the tines of a fork or your fingers. Line the tart shell(s) with aluminum foil and then fill with pie weights or beans. Bake in the preheated for 5 to 6 minutes. Remove from the oven and take out the pie weights and aluminum, prick the bottom of each shell with a fork and return to the oven until the shells are crisp and lightly browned, about 10 minutes longer. Remove the shell(s) and let them cool completely before filling.

Tart Filling

⅓ c	tart plum jelly		¼ c	sugar
¼ c	water		2 c	blackberries, or berries of your choice

Prepare the filling as follows: Combine jelly, sugar, water and 12 of the berries in a saucepan. Bring to a boil, crushing the berries with the back of a fork as the mixture heats. Continue cooking the mixture until it is thick enough to coat the back of a spoon without dripping off, about 10 minutes. Remove from the heat and let cool until warm.

With a pastry brush, paint the bottom of the tart shell(s) with the warm jelly mixture. Stack the berries as high as you like and drizzle each with about 1 T of the jelly mixture. Serve warm or cold in or out of the pans with a dollop of whipped cream or drizzled with vanilla flavored heavy cream.

Queen Assumed into Heaven, pray for us!

Queen of Peace, Our Lady of Fatima

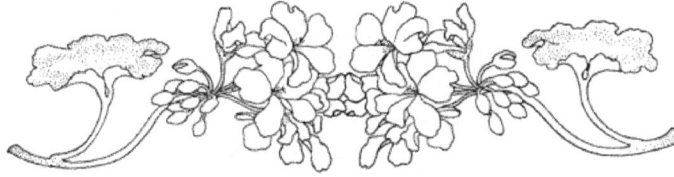

Queen of Peace, pray for us.

Our Lady of Fatima
May 13

"My Immaculate Heart will be your refuge and the way that will lead you to God." —Fatima, June 13, 1917

The Feast of Our Lady of Fatima commemorates the first day Our Lady appeared to three peasant children at Fatima, Portugal. On May 13, 1917 and then on the thirteenth of each month through October 1917, Mary appeared to Jacinta Marto, her brother Francesco, and Lucia Santos. In each of these six appearances, she asked them to pray for the reparation of all sinners, promising a special miracle during her final appearance so that all who saw would believe. She urged the children to ask the faithful to pray the Rosary and do penance as well so that the world would not be chastised for its many sins. On her first visit, Mary asked, *"Are you willing to offer yourselves to God and bear all the sufferings He wills to send you, as an act of reparation for the conversion of sinners?"*

Along with Jacinta, Francesco and Lucia, more than 100,000 people witnessed the miracle of the dancing sun at Fatima. The apparitions were officially declared authentic by the Bishops of Portugal in 1930. Here are the things requested by Our Lady in reparation for sin:

1. Consecration to her Immaculate Heart,
2. attending Mass for five first Saturdays of any five consecutive months,
3. offering daily sacrifices for the conversion of sinners, during those five consecutive months,
4. praying five decades of the Rosary each day, and
5. wearing the Brown Scapular as a sign of consecration to Mary.

Our Lady's main message at Fatima was to pray for peace and for those who do not have anyone else to pray for them. "Pray, pray a great deal and make sacrifices for sinners, for many souls go to hell because they have no one to pray and make sacrifices for them," she urged. This was considered Our Lady's Peace Plan for Heaven, and all that made an effort to live according to her requests mentioned above would have a good chance of achieving Heaven and contributing to peace in our families and our society. Because of Mary's grace and love for all her children, she is honored on this feast as Our Lady, Queen of Peace. In response to Mary's requests, Pope Pius XII consecrated the whole world to Mary's Immaculate Heart in 1942.

Teatime Chat

Today is a day for rejoicing in the goodness of Our Lord, praising Him for His mother Mary as revealed to the children at Fatima. Each time Mary appeared she spoke about what they were supposed to do for her. As she laid out her instructions, she assured the children that all she was asking of them would help to promote the peace and love in the world that was so lacking at that time in history.

Ask your children to think about a time when things were not so peaceful between their siblings and see if they can come up with some suggestions for resolving their disputes peacefully. For example, when Timmy "took away" Sarah's crayons without asking permission, was he being peaceful? Have them role-play how they might calmly and peacefully handle difficult situations. Remind them that part of their peace offerings should include asking Jesus and Mary for help. Then, if you create a family peace plan, you can encourage them to remember some of these ideas and gently point out how they can feel good about being part of Mary's requests for more peace and love in the world. Peace can start right in your own home!

Devotional Activities

♥ Our Lady's Dancing Sun

Supplies: Paper plates painted yellow, or pick up yellow plates at the party store, yellow construction paper cut into large narrow triangles to look like rays of the sun, glue stick, tape or stapler, gold glitter or glitter pens, real or silk flowers, holy cards of Mary or our Lady of Fatima with her gold crown.

Directions: Glue, tape or staple the pre-cut "sunrays" around the outside edge of your paper plates. Decorate with the glitter, pens, flowers and holy cards. These would be delightful hung from a chandelier or displayed on your Mary altar.

♥ *Fatima Peace Plan*

It would be fun to create a "Fatima Peace Plan" for your own family today! On poster board or scrapbook paper list what are some important ways to direct your family toward a peace plan. Be sure to have some stickers, markers and crayons available.

Since our main goal as Catholic parents is to help our children get to heaven, what better way than to instill good habits towards peace within the domestic church? After you have made your list for The "_____" Family Peace Plan, decorate and then hang it prominently in your home.

♥ Watch: *The Day the Sun Danced DVD*

The most exciting thing about your celebration today is that you have engaged your family in Our Lady's Peace Plan for heaven. Whether you are going to follow the specific requests she asked of the children at Fatima, or simply create your own action plan for peace, you have nonetheless instilled in them a devotion to Our Lady of Fatima.

If you have decided to begin the Windeatt *Our Lady of Fatima* book (see Appendix A)—or if your children are older, the *Vision* book—as a read aloud, teatime is a wonderful time to start. My children love to draw pictures and color during our read aloud times. Pull out some blank paper now, or give them the Fatima coloring book! Finish by praying a decade of the rosary for the fifth Glorious mystery, the crowning of Our Lady, *Queen of Peace.*

♥ Pray:

> *O Most Holy Virgin Mary, Queen of the most holy Rosary, you were pleased to appear to the children of Fatima and reveal a glorious message. We implore you, inspire in our hearts a fervent love for the recitation of the Rosary. By meditating on the mysteries of the redemption that are recalled therein may we obtain the graces and virtues that we ask, through the merits of Jesus Christ, our Lord and Redeemer.*

Teatime Recipe Idea

Devil's Food cupcakes with Mary's Mantle blue frosting

Choosing devil's food cake for your cupcake today represents the vision of hell shown to the children by Our Lady and the frosting is like Mary's mantle of grace covering over the sins of others. You can refer back to the plea she gave the children when she asked them to pray for sinners everywhere to promote world peace.

Steamed milk with honey

Gently heat milk over medium heat until just starting to scald, add 1 teaspoon of honey to each mug and pour in the warm milk, stir to mix and serve. If you have a hand held milk frother, use this to gently froth the milk and honey before serving.

Queen of Peace, pray for us!

Appendices

Appendix A

Recommended Reading

Children's Picture Books

Berger, Helen. *The Donkey's Dream*. Philomel Books, 1985 (OOP)

De Paola, Tomie. *Mary the Mother of Jesus*. Holiday House, 1995

De Paola, Tomie. *The Lady of Guadalupe*. Holiday House, New York, 1980

Joslin, Mary. *Mary, Mother of Jesus*. Loyola Press, 1999

Children's Chapter Books

Pauli, Hertha. *Bernadette: Our Lady's Servant*. Ignatius Press, 1999

Power-Waters, Alma. *St. Catherine Laboure and The Miraculous Medal*. Ignatius Press

Windeatt, Mary Fabian. *The Miraculous Medal: The Story of Our Lady's Appearances to St. Catherine Labouré*. Tan, 1993

Windeatt, Mary Fabian. *The Children of Fatima: Our Lady's Message to the World*. Tan, 1991

Children's Activity and Coloring Resources

Windeatt, Mary Fabian. *Our Lady of Fatima Coloring Book.* Tan Books

Recipe and Craft Idea Books

Cantrell, Alice. *Tea and Cake with the Saints.* Little Way Press, 2007

Cantrell, Alice. *Sewing With Saint Anne.* Little Way Press, 2002

Audio and Visual Resources

"*Bernadette: Princess of Lourdes*" DVD Creative Communications of America, 1993

"*The Day the Sun Danced*" DVD Creative Communications of America, 1997

"*Juan Diego, Messenger of Guadalupe*" DVD Creative Communications of America

"*The Song of Bernadette*" DVD 20th Century Fox, 1945

Poetry

Stevenson, Robert Louis. *Good and Bad Children from The Book of Virtues by William J. Bennett.* Simon & Schuster, 1993

Parent Resources

Bogle, Joanna. *A Book of Feasts and Seasons.* Gracewing, 2006

Buono, Anthony. *The Greatest Marian Titles: Their History, Meaning and Usage.* Alba House, 2008

Ghezzi, Bert. *Voices of the Saints.* Image Books, 2002

Gould, Meredith. *The Catholic Home: Celebrations and Traditions for Holidays, Feast Days, and Every Day.* Doubleday, 2004

Gunther, Alice. *Haystack Full of Needles: A Catholic Homeschoolers Guide to Socialization.* Pennsylvania, Hillside Press, 2008

Krymow, Vincenzina. *Mary's Flowers* St. Anthony's Messenger Press, 2002

Martin, Puccio & Romanowsky. *The Catholic Parent Book of Feasts: Celebrating the Church Year with your Family.* Our Sunday Visitor, 1999

McLouglin, Helen. *My Name Day: Come for Dessert.* The Liturgical Press, 1962

McNamara, Robinson, & Neuberger. *The Big Book of Catholic Customs and Traditions.* Our Sunday Visitor, 2003

Newland, Mary Reed. *The Year and Our Children.* Sophia Institute Press, 2007

Santorum, Karen. *Everyday Graces.* ISI Books, 2003

Vitz, Evelyn Birge. *A Continual Feast.* Ignatius, 1985

Appendix B

The Merry, Mary Month of May

This is a whole month dedicated to Our Lady as deemed by the Church with many ideas for you to share and celebrate with your children. Some or all of the activities will ensure that you will please Our Lady during her special month.

*Special Note: Please do not feel that you have to accomplish all of the devotions and activities in honor of Mary this month. Save some for the years to come.

1) Begin this special month with baskets filled with flowers and niceties to fill your May Cones, Baskets, Boxes, Cans or whatever you choose to use for May Day. A dance around a Maypole would top off the day ☺

2) May Crowning – make a fresh flower wreath for your Mary statues. Outside May coronations are especially lovely. Create a banner to be carried and process with someone carrying the special wreath and sing *Bring Flowers to the Rarest* (Appendix E) as you place the wreath on Mary's head. A decade of the rosary would be nice and then finish your celebration with some kind of treat or party to make the day extra special.

3) Lovely Lady Dressed in Blue – Poem for all to learn and recite with a lovely tea time including Blue Frosted Cupcakes or a Blueberry Coffeecake.

4) May Marian Altar – plan to have fresh flowers at Our Lady's altar all month long. Each child can take turns with this auspicious task. A holy water font, bowl or bottle would be nice to have close for daily blessings.

5) Make a list of all the Flowers for Mary with drawings.

6) Learn the Hymn – *'Tis the Month of Our Mother* (Appendix E)

7) Make a Marian Banner to be carried during the crowning; include some Marian symbols. This could also be an isolated activity if you are not able to do a Crowning.

8) Learn this beautiful prayer - To the Blessed Mother:
My Queen, My Mother, I give myself entirely to Thee, and to show my devotion to Thee, I consecrate to thee this day my eyes, my ears, my mouth, my heart, my entire self, without reserve. Wherefore, good Mother, as I am Thine own, keep me, defend me as Thy property and possession. Amen.

9) Make a Spiritual Bouquet for someone in the family, roll it into a scroll and tie it with a pretty ribbon and a flower. Fill a basket with these to hand out to friends after Mass.

10) Pray all the decades of the Rosary (all 20) try for one decade each day.

11) Make a Rose Garland to hang in your breakfast room to remember that Mary is remembered mainly in this flower. (Felt, Fabric or Origami work well for this).

12) Learn the Hymn *Daily, Daily Sing to Mary* (Appendix E).

13) Make a Garland of felt pouches numbered 1-31, Marian activity or treat inside (fashioned after Advent calendars)

14) Make a wreath out of Rosemary to remember Our Lady, or plant a Rosemary tree outside in your Mary Garden, rosemary is for remembrance.

15) Learn *The May Queen* poem by Alfred Lord Tennyson.

16) Think of making a special "Consecration to Mary" this month. Reading the book "True Devotion" by Saint Louis de Montfort will inspire you to think of this for a lifelong devotion to Mary and Jesus.

17) Look at beautiful Art appreciation sites for images of Mary throughout the ages. This would make a lovely Sunday afternoon activity for the whole family, Dad, too.

18) Learn the *Hail Holy Queen* in song, prayer or Latin. (Appendix E)

19) Create beautiful Holy Water fonts for Our Lady using items from around the house.

20) Make a pennant banner with the Seven Joys of Mary on each pennant, display in your altar area.

21) Write a poem about your Rosary.

22) Make Origami roses, create bouquets, garlands, or wreaths

23) Make miniature Marian Shrines from finished Tea Boxes or Café Tins

24) Create a special devotional prayer book, adding to it each day in May with your favorite Saint and Marian quotes.

25) Make a beautiful cake and decorate it with Candied Violets, invite friends to the Feast of the Visitation to finish out your Month of May celebrations.

Appendix C

Recommended Resources

References for Online Novena Prayers

A Treasury of Traditional Catholic Novenas:
www.fisheaters.com/novenas.html

Catholic Links: www.catholiclinks.org/novenasenglish.htm

EWTN: www.ewtn.com/Devotionals/prayers/novena.htm

Sources for Marian Statues

Leaflet Online: www.leafletonline.com

Mary Garden Ideas

Mary Gardens: www.mgardens.org/index

Brown Scapular Society and Consecration

Free Brown Scapular: www.freebrownscapular.com

Our Father's House

Mini Mass Kits, Catechesis of the Good Shepard, and Many other religious items and books: www.ourfathershouse.biz

Our Lady of Lourdes Grotto Kit

Illuminated Ink: www.illuminatedink.com

Other Grotto Kits

OL of Fatima, OL of Guadalupe, OL of the Snows

www.emmanuelbooks.com (302) 325-9515

Miscellaneous Marian Resources

Precious Mary Paper Dolls: www.emmanuelbooks.com (302) 325-9515

Rosary Coloring Book: www.emmanuelbooks.com

Mary Memory/Go to the Grotto Matching Card Game: www.emmanuelbooks.com

Mary Vitamin online prayers and meditations dedicated to the Blessed Virgin Mary http://groups.yahoo.com/group/MaryVitamin/

Additional Craft Resources

Lakeshore Learning for great supplies: www.lakeshorelearning.com

Art Appreciation Sites

Lib-Art www.lib-art.com/art.php?id=19046 (Assumption of Mary)

Web Gallery of Art www.wga.hu/index.html

Appendix D

Marian Hymns

Ave Maris Stella
Anonymous 9th century Latin hymn

Hail, O Star of the ocean,
God's own Mother blest,
ever sinless Virgin,
gate of heav'nly rest.

Taking that sweet Ave,
which from Gabriel came,
peace confirm within us,
changing Eve's name.

Break the sinners' fetters,
make our blindness day,
Chase all evils from us,
for all blessings pray.

Show thyself a Mother,
may the Word divine,
born for us thine Infant,
hear our prayers through thine.

Virgin all excelling,
mildest of the mild,
free from guilt preserve us
meek and undefiled.

Keep our life all spotless,
make our way secure
till we find in Jesus,
joy for evermore.

Praise to God the Father,
honor to the Son,
in the Holy Spirit,
be the glory one. Amen.

Stabat Mater Dolorosa

Bring Flowers to the Rarest
Anonymous

Bring flowers of the rarest
bring blossoms the fairest,
from garden and woodland and hillside and dale;
our full hearts are swelling,
our glad voices telling
the praise of the loveliest flower of the vale!

Refrain:
O Mary we crown thee with blossoms today!
Queen of the Angels and Queen of the May.
O Mary we crown thee with blossoms today,
Queen of the Angels and Queen of the May.

Their lady they name thee,
Their mistress proclaim thee,
Ah, grant that thy children on earth be as true
as long as the bowers
are radiant with flowers,
as long as the azure shall keep its bright hue
Refrain

Sing gaily in chorus;
the bright angels o'er us
re-echo the strains we begin upon earth;
their harps are repeating
the notes of our greeting,
for Mary herself is the cause of our mirth
Refrain

Those Five Wounds on Jesus smitten,

Traditional for Lent, Good Friday and
Stations of the Cross
Ascribed to Jacapone da Todi, d. 1306

At the Cross Her station keeping
Stood the mournful Mother weeping,
Close to Jesus to the last.

Through Her Heart, His sorrow sharing,
All His bitter anguish bearing,
Lo! the piercing sword had passed.

O how sad and sore distressed
Was that Mother, highly bleed,
Of the Sole-Begotten One.

Mournful, with Heart's prostration,
Mother meek, the bitter Passion
Saw She of Her glorious Son.

Who on Christ's dear Mother gazing,
In Her trouble so amazing,
Born of woman, would not weep?

Who on Christ's dear Mother thinking,
Such a cup of sorrow drinking,
Would not share Her sorrow deep?

For His people's sins rejected,
Saw Her Jesus unprotected.
Saw with thorns, with scourges rent.

Saw Her Son from judgement taken,
Her Beloved in death forsaken,
Till His Spirit forth He sent.

Fount of love and holy sorrow,
Mother, may my spirit borrow
Somewhat of Your woe profound.

Unto Christ with pure emotion,
Raise my contrite heart's devotion,
To read love in every wound.

Mother! in my heart be written,
Deep as in Your own they be.

You, Your Savior's Cross did bare,
You, Your Son's rebuke did share.
Let me share them both with Thee.

In the Passion of my Maker,
Be my sinful soul partaker,
Weep 'til death and weep with You.

Mine with You be that sad station,
There to watch the great salvation,
Wrought upon the atoning Tree.

Virgin, you of virgins fairest,
May the bitter woe Thou bearest
Make on me impression deep.

Thus Christ's dying may I carry,
With Him in His Passion tarry,
And His Wounds in memory keep.

May His Wound both wound and heal
me,
He enkindle, cleanse, strengthen me,
By His Cross my hope and stay.

May He, when the mountains quiver,
From that flame which burns forever,
Shield me on the Judgement Day.

Jesus, may Your Cross defend me,
And Your Mother's prayer befriend me;
Let me die in Your embrace.

When to dust my dust returns,
Grant a soul, that to You yearns,
In Your paradise a place. Amen.

'Tis the Month of Our Mother

'Tis the month of our Mother
The blessed and beautiful days,
When our lips and our spirits,
are glowing with love and with praise.

Refrain:
All Hail! to thee, dear Mary,
the guardian of our way;
To the fairest of Queens,
Be the fairest of seasons, sweet May.

Oh! what peace to her children,
mid sorrows and trials to know,
that the love of their Mother,
Hath ever a solace for woe.

And, what joy to the erring,
The sinful and sorrowful soul;
That a trust in her guidance,
will lead to a glorious goal.

Let us sing then, rejoicing,
that God hath so honored our race,
as to clothe with our nature,
Sweet Mary, the Mother of Grace.

Salve, Regina
Hermannus Contractus 1013-1054
(Herman the Cripple)

Salve, Regina, mater misericordiae;
vita, dulcedo et spes nostra, salve.
Ad te clamamus exsules filii Hevae.
Ad te suspiramus gementes et flentes
in hac lacrimarum valle.
Eia ergo, advocata nostra, illos tuos
misericordes oculos ad nos converte.
Et Iesum, benedictum fructum ventris tui,
nobis post hoc exsilium ostende.
O clemens, o pia, o dulcis Virgo Maria.

Hail Holy Queen Enthroned Above
Aimor, Bishop of Le Puy, 11th century

Hail, Holy Queen enthroned above, O Maria!
Hail, Mother of mercy and of love, O Maria!
Triumph all ye cherubim!
Sing with us ye seraphim!
Heaven and earth resound the hymn!
Salve, salve, salve, Regina!

Our life, our sweetness here below, O Maria!
Our hope in sorrow and in woe, O Maria!
Triumph all ye cherubim!
Sing with us ye seraphim!
Heaven and earth resound the hymn!
Salve, salve, salve, Regina!

To thee do we cry, poor sons of Eve, O Maria!
To thee we sigh, we mourn, we grieve, O Maria!
Triumph all ye cherubim!
Sing with us ye seraphim!
Heaven and earth resound the hymn!
Salve, salve, salve, Regina!

Turn, then, most gracious Advocate, O Maria!
Towards us thine eyes compassionate, O Maria!
Triumph all ye cherubim!
Sing with us ye seraphim!
Heaven and earth resound the hymn!
Salve, salve, salve, Regina! O Maria!

When this our exile is complete, O Maria!
Show us thy Son, our Jesus sweet, O Maria!
Triumph all ye cherubim!
Sing with us ye seraphim!
Heaven and earth resound the hymn!
Salve, salve, salve, Regina!

O clement, gracious Mother sweet, O Maria!
O virgin Mary we entreat, O Maria!
Triumph all ye cherubim!
Sing with us ye seraphim!
Heaven and earth resound the hymn!
Salve, salve, salve, Regina!

Daily, Daily, Sing to Mary
Ascribed to St Bernard of Cluny, d. 1150

Daily, daily sing to Mary,
Sing, my soul, her praises due.
All her feasts, her actions worship
With the heart's devotion true.
Lost in wond'ring contemplation,
Be her Majesty confess'd.
Call her Mother, call her Virgin,
Happy Mother, Virgin blest.

She is mighty to deliver.
Call her, trust her lovingly.
When the tempest rages round thee,
She will calm the troubled sea.
Gifts of heaven she has given,
Noble Lady, to our race.
She, the Queen, who decks her subjects
With the light of God's own grace.

Sing, my tongue, the Virgin's trophies
Who for us her Maker bore.
For the curse of old inflicted,
Peace and blessing to restore.
Sing in songs of peace unending,
Sing the world's majestic Queen.
Weary not nor faint in telling.
All the gifts she gives to men.

On This Day, O Beautiful Mother

Refrain:
On this day, O Beautiful Mother!
On this day we give thee our love;
Near thee, Madonna, fondly we hover,
trusting thy gentle care to prove.

On this day we ask to share,
dearest Mother, thy sweet care;
Aid us e'er, our feet astray,
wandering from thy guiding way.
Refrain

Queen of Angels, deign to hear,
thy dear children's humble prayer;
Young hearts gain, O Virgin pure,
sweetly to thyself allure.
Refrain

Immaculate Mary
Anonymous, Lourdes Hymn

Immaculate Mary, your praises we sing;
You reign now in splendor with Jesus our King.
Ave, ave, ave, Maria! Ave, ave, Maria!

In heaven, the blessed your glory proclaim;
On earth we, your children,
invoke your sweet name.
Ave, ave, ave, Maria! Ave, ave, Maria!

We pray for the Church, our true Mother on earth,
And beg you to watch o'er the land of our birth.
Ave, ave, ave, Maria! Ave, ave, Maria!

Appendix E

Chronological Order of Celebrations

Activities keyed to the calendar year feast day.

January

February

March

April

May

June

July

August

September

October

November

December

Appendix F — Recipes

Annunciation Waffles

The waffles can be served at breakfast or as a special dessert.

1 ¾ c	heavy cream		¼ t	salt
1 ⅓ c.	all purpose flour		½ c	cold water
2 T	sugar		3-4 T	melted sweet-cream butter

Directions: Whip the cream until stiff. Mix the flour, sugar, salt in a bowl. Stir in the water to make a smooth batter. Fold in the whipped cream, then stir in the melted butter.

Cook waffles according to your manufacturers waffle maker until crisp. Place on a rack to keep crisp while the others cook. Serve with fresh fruit, syrup and more whipped cream. Alternatively these would be lovely drizzled with melted chocolate!

Baked Apples with Raisins and Nuts

(These will be even more tempting than the "one" Adam and Eve ate)

6-8 Large Tart Apples such as Macintosh
    (or enough for each person to have ½ an apple)
Chopped Walnuts or Pecans, Raisins
Whipped Cream (optional)

⅔ c.   brown sugar, packed
½ t   ground ginger
1 t   cinnamon

Directions: Preheat oven to 350°F. Core the apples to within ½ inch of the bottom of the apple, but not through. Combine all the ingredients except the whipped cream and fill each apple cavity packing in gently to the top. Dot each top with butter and place into a baking pan and fill with hot water. Cover and bake about 45 minutes or until the apples and tender, but not applesauce ☺. Let cool slightly, then slice each apple in half and discard bottom core parts. Serve warm with a dollop of whip cream and a dusting of cinnamon.

Blackberry Tarts

(or a combination of summer berries of your choice)

For the Tart Shells: (You can buy these pre-made if you prefer)

2 c	all purpose flour		½ c	unsalted butter, chilled
1 t	salt		3 T	margarine, chilled
			6 T	ice water

Directions: To make the tart shells, sift the flour and salt together into a bowl. Cut the butter and margarine into ½ inch chunks and add them to the flour mixture. Blend with a pastry blender until pea-sized balls form. Add the ice water 1 T at a time. After each addition of water, turn with a fork and then your fingertips. This will help to keep the pastry light and flaky. Try not to overwork the dough or it will become tough. Gather the dough into a ball and wrap in plastic wrap to chill for about 15 minutes.

Preheat the oven to 350°F. On a lightly floured work surface, roll out the dough to ⬚ of an inch thick. Lift dough into the tart pan(s) and press gently to shape it into the pan. You can mold the edges with the tines of a fork or your fingers. Line the tart shell(s) with aluminum foil and then fill with pie weights or beans. Bake in the preheated for 5 to 6 minutes. Remove from the oven and take out the pie weights and aluminum, prick the bottom of each shell with a fork and return to the oven until the shells are crisp and lightly browned, about 10 minutes longer. Remove the shell(s) and let them cool completely before filling.

Tart Filling

⅓ c	tart plum jelly		¼ c	sugar
¼ c	water		2 c	blackberries, or berries of your choice

Prepare the filling as follows: Combine jelly, sugar, water and 12 of the berries in a saucepan. Bring to a boil, crushing the berries with the back of a fork as the mixture heats. Continue cooking the mixture until it is thick enough to coat the back of a spoon without dripping off, about 10 minutes. Remove from the heat and let cool until warm.

With a pastry brush, paint the bottom of the tart shell(s) with the warm jelly mixture. Stack the berries as high as you like and drizzle each with about 1 T of the jelly mixture. Serve warm or cold in or out of the pans with a dollop of whipped cream or drizzled with vanilla flavored heavy cream.

Bûche de Noël

*Special Note: This is a rather involved teatime treat, albeit lovely and traditional for Christmas; it may be more than you want to tackle. Feel free to substitute your own traditional holiday fare here, or even purchase a lovely *Bûche* at your local bakery. I've even been known to pull out a box of Twinkies and coat them with chocolate sauce.

¾ c	cake flour		¾ c	sugar
¾ t	baking powder		¼ t	salt
¼ t	salt		1 t	vanilla extract
5	eggs, separated into 2 bowls			

Directions: Preheat oven to 400°F and prepare a 10 ½ × 15 ½ × 1-inch jelly roll pan by greasing it, lining it with waxed or parchment paper, and then greasing it as well. Also have ready a larger sheet pan and a clean linen dish towel.

Sift together the flour, baking powder and salt, set aside. Beat the egg yolks until thick and pale. Gradually add six tablespoons of the sugar, beating well after each addition; the mixture should fall into a thick ribbon when the beaters are lifted. Add the vanilla and beat again.

With clean dry beaters, beat the egg whites until foamy. Gradually add the remaining sugar, beating constantly, until the whites stand in firm, glossy, moist peaks. Fold a third of the whites into the yolk mixture to lighten it; fold the rest of the egg whites into the lightened yolk mixture.

Using a fine strainer, gradually sift the dry ingredients into the egg mixture, folding them in gently but thoroughly. Spread the batter evenly in the prepared pan, making sure to get it into the corners. Put the pan in the oven immediately.

Bake for 10-12 minutes, or just until the cake is golden on top and tester inserted in the center comes out clean. Do not over bake.

Working quickly, cover the pan first with the dishtowel and then with the cookie sheet. Turn over the cookie sheet, towel and pan to turn out the cake. Remove the smaller cookie sheet that you baked on and then peel off the parchment paper. Slide the towel and cake onto the counter or table; the cake is wrong side up. Cut off any crisp edges, fold one end of the towel over the short end of the cake and roll up the cake in the towel. Place the cake seam-side down onto a wire rack to cool completely. (See frosting recipes below before proceeding with the rest).

Unroll the cooled cake leaving it on the towel and spread ½ cup of the Mocha Silk Frosting evenly over the cake, all the way to the edges. Spread 2 cups of the Buttercream Frosting over the thin layer of mocha pushing a generous amount into the curved end. Roll up again without the towel but using the towel to help guide your roll. Place cake seam side down on a cake plate or tray. Use a small spatula to remove any excess filling from the ends and seam edge. Refrigerate for about an hour to firm the filling.

Trim and taste ☺ a thin slice from the end of the chilled cake; cut and reserve a wedge from the other end. Spread a little leftover butter cream on the top of the cake and press the reserved wedge into it to make a "knothole."

Now frost the entire cake with the remaining mocha silk frosting building the frosting up around the sides of the knothole leaving the top free of frosting. Repeatedly draw a narrow spatula lengthwise through the frosting to simulate the rough texture of the bark. Decorate as desired to make your bûche de noël, as "log-like" as desired.

Buttercream Frosting

½ c	superfine sugar		7-8 T	heavy cream
1	egg yolk		½ c + 2T	butter, softened
pinch	salt		2 ⅓ c	sifted confectioners' sugar
1 ½ t	vanilla extract			

Directions: Combine the sugar, egg yolk, salt, vanilla and 2 ½ tablespoons of the cream and beat for eight minutes at medium speed in the bowl of an electric mixer. In a large bowl, cream ½ cup of the butter until light. Add the yolk mixture a little at a time, beating well after each addition. Gradually add two cups of the confectioners' sugar, beating well after each addition. Makes 2 ½ to 3 cups frosting.

Mocha Silk Frosting

1¾ c	confectioners' sugar		1 ½ T	light corn syrup
3 T	unsweetened cocoa powder		1 t	vanilla extract
2 t	powdered instant coffee		2-4 T	heavy cream
5 ⅓ T	butter, softened			

Directions: Sift together and then stir the sugar, cocoa and coffee. Add the butter, corn syrup, vanilla and two tablespoons cream and beat for a minute at medium speed. Add just enough of the remaining cream to make the frosting easy to spread.

Chocolate Ganache Cake

For the Cake -

2	sticks unsalted butter, softened
1 c	sugar
4	extra large eggs, room temperature
1	16 oz. can Hershey's chocolate syrup
1 T	pure vanilla extract
1 c	all purpose flour

For the Ganache –

½ c	heavy cream
8 oz.	semisweet chocolate chips
1 t	instant coffee granules optional

Directions: Preheat oven to 325°F. Butter and flour an 8-inch round cake pan lined with parchment paper, or alternatively use an 8-inch *spring form* pan. Cream the butter and sugar together until light and fluffy. Add the eggs, one at a time, mixing after each addition. Mix in the chocolate syrup and vanilla. Add the flour and mix until just combined. Be careful not to over beat or the cake will be tough. Pour the batter into the pan and bake for 40 to 45 minutes, or until just set in the middle. Let cool thoroughly in the pan.

For the *ganache*, cook the heavy cream, chocolate chips, and coffee granules in the top of a double boiler over simmering water until smooth and warm, stirring occasionally. Place the cake upside down on a wire rack situated on a cookie sheet and pour the ganache over the cake evenly. Make sure to cover both the cake and sides. You can tilt the rack to smooth the glaze. Serve immediately. You could also decorate with shiny silver *dragees* that can be found at cake decorating or craft stores!

Deviled Worms

Serve gummy worms immersed in flavored gelatin to emphasize Mary crushing the head of the serpent. Juice would work well today! Alternatively, your favorite recipe for Deviled Eggs served with a spear and an olive might be a nice touch. Here's one we like:

Deviled Eggs

1-2 dozen	hard-boiled eggs	½ - 1 c	mayonnaise
1 ½ t	salt	2-3 T	Dijon-style mustard
1 t	freshly cracked pepper	Paprika for garnish, black olives	

Directions: Peel hard-boiled eggs and slice in two. Remove yolks and place in a bowl. Add all ingredients except garnishes and combine until smooth. A fork works well for this. Scoop yolk mixture into halved whites, dust with paprika and place a speared olive through the top of each.

Divinity Candy

½ c	granulated sugar	½ c	water
¼ t	salt	2	large egg whites, room
½ c	light corn syrup		temp.
		1 t	vanilla extract

Directions: Be sure to make divinity on a dry day; candy will not harden on a humid day. In a medium saucepan over medium high heat, heat sugar, salt, syrup and water to boiling, stirring constantly until sugar is dissolved. Set candy thermometer in place and continue cooking over medium low heat, not stirring, until the temperature reaches 266°F. When the temperature reaches 260°F beat the egg whites with electric mixer at high speed, until stiff peaks form. While beating, pour the hot syrup slowly into the egg whites. Beat for about 2 to 3 minutes, until mixture isn't glossy. Add vanilla and turn to low speed. Continue beating until the mixture holds its shape when dropped from a spoon. It will probably be too thick for the mixer at this point. With a lightly buttered teaspoon, drop onto waxed paper. Work as quickly as possible. If mixture gets too thick to work with, add a few drops of water. Let stand until dry. Store in tightly covered containers. Enjoy, it will be divine!

Favorite Brownies

½ c	butter	2 c	sugar
4 oz.	Unsweetened chocolate	1 t	vanilla extract
4	eggs, room temperature	1 c	sifted all-purpose flour
¼ t	salt		confectioners' sugar for garnish

Directions: Preheat oven to 350°F. Melt butter and chocolate in microwave or in a bowl over a simmering pan on the stove. Let mixture cool. Beat the eggs and salt until light yellow and gradually add the sugar and vanilla. Beat until well creamed. Combine the cooled chocolate mixture and the egg mixture and fold in the flour, stir until smooth. Pour into a greased 9 × 13-inch pan and bake for approximately 25 minutes. Do not over bake so the brownies remain chewy. Let cool before cutting. Enjoy with powdered sugar sprinkled on top!

Favorite Flan

½ c	sugar		1	14 oz. can sweetened
3	Eggs			condensed milk
2 c	whole milk		1 T	vanilla extract

Directions: Preheat oven to 375°F; have ready a one-quart baking dish and a kettle of boiling water. Cook the sugar in a small, heavy pan over medium heat for several minutes, stirring constantly, until all the sugar melts and turns a golden brown. Be careful not to let it burn. Immediately pour the caramelized sugar into the baking dish and tilt the dish to coat the bottom and sides. Set aside.

In a large bowl, beat the remaining ingredients until well blended. Pour the mixture into the baking dish, right onto the caramelized sugar.

Place the baking dish in a larger pan on the middle rack of the oven. Pull the rack out far enough to fill the larger pan with an inch of boiling water. Slowly push the rack back in and bake for approximately 70 minutes, or until a knife inserted in the center of the custard comes out clean.

Let the flan cool for an hour, then cover with plastic wrap and refrigerate overnight. Before serving, run a knife around the outside edge of the flan to loosen it from the baking dish. Cover tightly with an inverted serving dish and turn over to unmold.

Gingerbread Tea Cake

1 ½ c	unbleached all purpose flour	2 t	ground ginger
¼ c	sugar	¼ c	melted butter, cooled
1 t	baking powder	1 egg	beaten slightly
¼ t	baking soda	½ c	buttermilk
¼ t	salt	½ c	molasses
1 t	cinnamon	confectioners' sugar and whipped	
¼ t	each grated nutmeg & ground cloves	cream for garnish (optional)	

Directions: Butter and flour an 8″ or 9″ spring form pan with removable bottom or an 8″ square baking pan. Preheat oven to 350°. In a large mixing bowl combine flour, sugar, salt, baking powder, soda and spices. Add the milk, melted butter, egg, and molasses and beat with an electric mixer on low speed or by hand until well combined. Pour the batter into your greased and floured pan. Bake for 25-35 minutes or until a toothpick inserted into the center of the cake comes out clean. Let the cake cool for 15 minutes in the pan, and then remove and let cool completely on a wire cooling rack. When the cake is completely cool, dust with powdered sugar and serve with a dollop of whip cream if you wish.

Homemade Lemonade

3 ½ c	water	2 c	fresh lemon juice (squeezed from about 10 large lemons)
1 ½ c	sugar		

Directions: Bring water and sugar to a boil in a small saucepan, stirring occasionally until sugar dissolves. Let cool. Mix sugar syrup and lemon juice in a tall pitcher and stir to combine. Taste for tartness. If too tart, make some more syrup, or add a little honey to sweeten. Makes approximately 6 cups. Enjoy.

Ice Cream Mountains with Carmel Sauce and Clouds of Cream

Serve mounded vanilla ice cream and drizzle with warmed caramel sauce and top with a cloud of whipped cream. The whip cream and caramel can be store bought or here is a delectable recipe for caramel, so good you have to try it at least once.

For the Caramel:

1 ½ c   sugar
1 ¼ c   heavy cream
½ t   pure vanilla extract

Optional: chopped pecans to sprinkle on top!

Directions: Mix ⬚ c water and the sugar in a medium heavy-bottomed saucepan. Cook without stirring, over low heat for 5 to 10 minutes, until sugar dissolves. Increase the heat to medium and boil uncovered until the sugar turns a warm chestnut brown color (about 350°F on a candy thermometer), 5 to 8 minutes, gently swirling the pan to stir the mixture. Be careful; the mixture is extremely hot! Watch it constantly at the end, as it will go from caramel to burned very quickly. Turn of the heat. Slowly add the cream, and be extra careful of spatters, then add the vanilla. The cream will bubble vigorously and the caramel will solidify; simmer over low heat, stirring constantly until the caramel dissolves and is smooth, about 2 to 3 minutes. Allow sauce to cool to room temperature, and it will thicken as it sits in about 2 to 3 hours.

Immaculate Heart Window Cookies

Here is a basic "*Linzer*" cookie recipe:

3 sticks	unsalted butter, room temperature		3 ½ c	all purpose flour
1 c	sugar		¼ t	salt
1 t	vanilla extract		¾ c	raspberry preserves
				Confectioners' sugar for dusting

Directions: Preheat oven to 350°F. In the bowl of an electric mixer fitted with the paddle attachment, mix together the butter and sugar until they are just combined. Add the vanilla. In another bowl, sift together the flour and salt, then add them to the butter mixture on low speed. When the dough starts to come together dump out onto a surface dusted with flour and shape into flat disc. Wrap in plastic and chill for 20 to 30 minutes.

Roll the dough ¼ inch thick and cut with a 3 – 4 heart shaped cookie cutter. Cut an equal number of the hearts with a smaller cutter to make the "window" pieces. Place all the cookies onto a cookie sheet and chill again for another 15 minutes or so. Bake the cookies for 20 – 25 minutes until the edges begin to just brown. Allow to cool to room temperature. Spread the raspberry preserves on the whole cookies and top with a "window" gently pressing the cookie into the jam. Dust with confectioners sugar if desired. Serve on a plate surrounded by rose petals to represent Our Lady's Immaculate Heart!

Merciful Blueberry Muffins

1 ¾ c	cake flour		¼ c	sour cream
2 t	baking soda		1 stick	unsalted butter, room temperature
1 t	cream of tartar		⅔ c.	butter
1 t	salt		1 large egg, room temperature	
1 pint	fresh blueberries		1 large egg yolk, room temperature	
¾ c	milk			

Directions: Preheat oven to 425°F. Butter or spray 18 muffin cups or line them with paper baking cups. Sift together the cake flour, soda, salt, and cream of tartar, twice. Remove a tablespoon or two of the dry ingredients to toss with the blueberries. In a separate bowl, stir the milk and sour cream together and set aside until needed.

   In a mixer fitted with the paddle attachment, beat the butter on medium speed until white and pale, about 3 minutes. Add the sugar and beat until the mixture no longer feels grainy, about 3 minutes, scrape down the paddle and the sides of the bowl as needed. Add the eggs and yolk and beat until the mixture if fluffy, about 2 to 3 minutes.

   Remove the bowl from the mixer and sift half of the dry ingredients into the bowl, add half of the mild and sour cream mixture and fold gently together, stopping when barely combined. Add the remaining dry and liquid mixtures and fold again just until combined. Sprinkle over the blueberries and barely fold them in as well.

   Spoon the batter into the prepared muffin tins, filling each cup at least two-thirds full and bake for 18 to 20 minutes or until the tops, which will be flat, are golden and spring back when lightly pressed. Turn out onto a cooling rack and let cool for 10 to 15 minutes before serving. Enjoy with fresh strawberries and cream for a deliciously merciful treat!

Mexican Hot Chocolate with Whipped Cream

½ c	sugar		4 c	milk
¼ c	Cocoa powder		¾ t	vanilla extract
Dash	salt		¼ t	cinnamon plus extra for dusting the whipped cream
⅓ c.	hot water			

Directions for stovetop cocoa for six servings: Mix sugar, cocoa and salt in a saucepan, stir in hot water. Cook and stir over medium heat until mixture boils, boil and stir 2 minutes. Stir in milk and heat gently over low heat, do NOT BOIL again. Remove from heat, stir in vanilla and cinnamon. Pour into cups top with whipped cream and dust with cinnamon!

Morning Biscuits with Rosemary

1½ c	unbleached flour		1 T	sugar
½ c	whole wheat flour		¾ c	milk
1 t	baking powder		2 T	butter
½ t	baking soda		2 t	crumbled, dried rosemary
dash	salt			(or 2 T fresh, chopped)

Excluding the rosemary, sift dry ingredients together in a large bowl. With a fork or pastry cutter, work the butter into the dry ingredients, some small lumps will remain. Add the rosemary and milk and mix well to form a soft dough.

Roll out the dough to ½ inch thickness on a lightly floured surface. Cut into 2 inch rounds and place on a greased and lightly floured baking sheet. Bake for 20 minutes at 400°F. Makes about 1½ dozen.

Serve with Rosemary Tea sweetened with honey.

Mystical Rose Basket Cupcakes

Baked cupcakes (any flavor you desire) white frosting , red fruit leather or roll-ups shaped into roses

red rope licorice (for basket handle) coconut pre-colored green (you can do this in a zip-topped bag with a few drops of green food coloring, shake to mix)

Directions: Assemble and enjoy with rose red fruit punch in pretty glasses or teacups! See photo below for an example, have fun!

Nutella® Ladyfingers

Package of Ladyfingers (check your market)
Nutella® or melted chocolate chip morsels
Flaked coconut, preferably unsweetened

Milk
Vanilla extract
honey

Directions: Dip the Ladyfingers into Nutella® or melted chocolate chips, and then roll them in the coconut.

Make the Vanilla Milk Tea by heating the milk just to scalding and adding a ¼ teaspoon of vanilla extract and 1 Tablespoon honey, stir to combine and serve in pretty mugs or teacups.

Perfect Scones

Representing the Perfections of Mary
(As perfected and offered by my dear daughter Emma Grace)

2 c	all purpose flour	6 T	butter, chilled & cut into chunks
1 T	baking powder		
2 T	sugar	¼ c	melted butter
½ t	salt		
½ c	buttermilk		Cinnamon sugar for topping

Directions: Mix together all the dry ingredients. Cut in the chilled butter chunks with your fingertips or a pastry blender. Mixture should resemble coarse cornmeal. Make a well in the dry ingredients and pour in buttermilk. Mix until just combined. Pour out dough onto a floured surface and gently press dough into a ½ inch round disc. Cut into 8 triangles (or other desired shape); brush the tops with the melted butter and sprinkle with cinnamon sugar. Bake at 425°F for 15 to 20 minutes or until lightly golden.

Pie Crust Tilmas with Cinnamon Sugar

Directions: Purchase pre-made piecrusts in your refrigerator section at the grocery store. Cut into a "tilma" shape and brush with melted butter, then sprinkle with cinnamon sugar. Bake at 350°F for about 7-10 minutes or until golden brown. Let cool slightly before serving.

Seven Herb Soup

*Special Note – Today rather than a sweet treat for teatime, I am recommending a special "*Seven Herb Soup*" as a luncheon that is traditionally served during Lent, but is totally appropriate for a Marian Feast.

2 c	potatoes, peeled and diced	spinach, chicory, green onions,
2 c	leeks, washed, sliced	collards, kale, mustard and turnip
½ c	heavy cream	greens,
2	quarts chicken broth	Salt
1 to 2 c	mixed chopped greens	White pepper to taste
	watercress, broccoli, broccolini,	1 lemon juiced
	broccoli rabe, beet greens, or	Parsley chopped for garnish
	dandelion greens	

Directions: Place the potatoes, leeks and broth in a large saucepan. Add 1 t salt and bring to a boil. Simmer, partly covered for about 20 minutes or until the potatoes and leeks are tender. Add the greens and simmer for 5 to 10 minutes longer, or until the greens have just become tender.

Puree the mixture in a blender or food processor, adding the heavy cream as you blend.

Pour the soup into a serving bowl or tureen. Add the white pepper to taste and the lemon juice. Taste for seasoning. If you plan to serve the soup cold, over salt it slightly. If the soup seems too thick, add a little chicken broth or if it's too thin, add some more heavy cream. Chill for several hours. I love this soup hot too and for this luncheon, it will be ready in no time! Serve with thick sliced French bread or rolls.

*Also note that if you want to stick to a teatime event, then you can simply have:
Black or Herbal Tea – no milk or sugar, or alternatively choose water

Shortbread "Host" Cookies

3 sticks	unsalted butter, softened		3 ½ c	all purpose flour
1 c	sugar		¼ t	salt
1 t	pure vanilla extract			

Directions: Mix butter and sugar by hand or in a mixer until just combined. Add the vanilla. Sift together the flour and the salt, then add them to the butter and sugar mixture until the dough just comes together. Dump onto a floured surface and gently shape into a disc and wrap in plastic to chill in the fridge for about a half hour.

Roll the dough about ½ inch thick and cut with a 2-inch round cutter. Place on an un-greased cutter sheet and bake for about 20 to 25 minutes until the edges are just beginning to brown. Cool to room temperature. If desired decorate with a cross motif with either a dusting of chocolate powder or melted chocolate chips drizzled atop.

Serve with grape or cranberry juice in tiny goblets if you have them to represent Jesus' blood.

Snowballs

1 c	butter		1 t	vanilla
½ c	powdered sugar		2 c	ground pecans
1 t	baking powder		2 c	flour

Directions: Mix all ingredients and refrigerate for an hour. Roll into balls and bake on a greased cookie sheet at 350°F for 15-18 minutes. While still hot from the oven roll in 2 cups powder sugar. Let cool and then roll again, enjoy!

St. Anne's Bird's Nests

Melt 12 oz. Chocolate morsels/chips over a simmering double boiler until smooth, stirring occasionally. Pour cooled chocolate over plain chow-mien noodles until completely covered. Spread spoonfuls of the chocolate noodles onto wax paper covered cookie sheet and use your fingers to form little nests. Fill with a few jellybeans for eggs and you have some sweet and adorable bird nests.

Star Anise Cookies

2 T	star anise pieces	2 T	balsamic vinegar
½ c	sugar	¼ c	all purpose flour
5 T	unsalted butter		

Directions: Preheat oven to 350°F and line 2 large baking sheets with parchment paper. In a sturdy mortar and pestle, grind the whole star anise pods until fine. Alternately you can use an electric coffee/spice grinder to finely grind star anise. In a 1 to 1 ½ quart heavy saucepan bring anise, sugar, butter, and vinegar to a boil over moderate heat, stirring, and boil 1 minute. Remove pan from heat and stir in flour and a pinch salt until mixture is smooth. Cool dough to room temperature.

Form and bake cookies as directed at below: Roll level ½ t dough into balls and arrange 4 inches apart on baking sheets. Bake cookies in batches in upper and lower thirds of oven, switching position of sheets halfway through baking, 10 minutes, or until cookies are flat and golden. Transfer parchment with cookies to racks to cool. Cool baking sheets and line with fresh parchment between batches.

Tart Tatin (Apple Crostata)

¼ t	kosher salt	1 ½ lbs	McIntosh, Gala or Empire Apples, peeled, cored and sliced or chunked
¼ t	cinnamon	¼ t	grated orange or lemon zest
⅛ t	allspice	¼ c	all purpose flour
4 T	cold unsalted butter, diced	¼ c	granulated or superfine sugar
2 T	melted butter		One Box Refrigerated Pie Crusts (2 in a box)

Directions: Roll out each pastry into a large circle (about 11 inches). Make sure they do not tear. Place each pastry onto a cookie sheet or sheet lined with parchment. Brush lightly with melted butter.

For the filling: Toss sliced or chunked apples with the orange or lemon zest. Place apples onto the tart dough leaving about a 1½ inch border.

Combine the flour, sugar, salt, cinnamon, and allspice in the bowl. Cut in the butter until the mixture is crumbly. Sprinkle evenly over the apples. Gently fold the border over the apples, pleating it to make a circle.

Bake at 425°F for 20 to 25 minutes or until crust is golden brown and the apples are tender, but not mushy. Let cool on wire rack for 5 minutes, then serve sliced thick with ice cream, whip cream or a drizzle of Carmel sauce. Enjoy!

Tea Cake with Candied/Sugared Violets

1 ½ c	cake flour	2/3 c	whole milk
¾ c	sugar	½ c	butter, softened
1½ t	baking powder	2	large eggs, lightly beaten
¼ t	salt	1½ t	pure vanilla extract

Directions: Preheat oven to 375°F. In a large mixing bowl, combine the flour, sugar, baking powder and salt. Add to this mixture the milk, softened butter, eggs and vanilla. Beat on low speed in an electric mixer until combined, then beat on medium for another minute. This step can also be done by hand. Pour the batter into a greased and floured 8️ to 9️ *spring form* pan or regular cake pan. Bake for approximately 25 minutes or until a wooden stick inserted into the center comes out clean and the top in golden brown. Let the cake cool on a wire rack for 15 minutes in the pan, and then remove the *spring form* sides and bottom and let cool completely on a plate. Dust with Confectioners' sugar and decorate the top and around the bottom of the cake (on the plate) with the Sugared Violets.

To make the Sugared Violets: You will need one bunch of violets, granulated sugar, one egg white, and a small paint brush.

Gather violets early in the day, or find them at the market (usually in the herb section). Whip the egg white until frothy. Working over a plate of granulated sugar, paint each violet with the egg white and carefully lay each violet in the sugar. Sprinkle more sugar on top and allow to dry on the plate. These lovely little treats can be used to decorate any dessert or used as a garnish on a plate of delicious items.

"Tower of David" Irish Soda Bread

4 c	unbleached all purpose flour	1 ½ t	kosher salt
1 t	baking soda	2 c	buttermilk

Directions: Preheat oven to 375°F. Grease an 8-inch iron skillet, a glass pie plate, or baking sheet and set aside. Mix the flour, baking soda, and salt into a bowl and stir to combine. Add the buttermilk and stir vigorously until the dough comes together. Then turn the dough out onto a lightly floured surface and gently knead for a minute. Do not overwork the dough as it will become tough. Pat the dough into a disk about 6 to 8 inches across and slash an "x" about ½ inch deep across the top. Place into your prepared baking pan and bake for about 50 minutes or until the bread is golden brown and the "x" has widened a bit. Transfer to a cooling rack, then slice and serve! It is most delectable served warm with a meal or tea. A funny note on storing if there is any leftover that by the end of the day it will be as hard as the "blarney stone" due to the tiny amount of fat in the buttermilk.

Wedding Cupcakes

Bake white cupcakes and let the children have fun creating their own "wedding cakes" for Mary and Joseph. We like a white cream cheese icing sprinkled with coconut!

Cream Cheese Icing

1	pound cream cheese, softened
2	sticks butter, softened
½ t	coconut extract
1 t	pure vanilla

1-2 pounds confectioners' sugar, depending on how thick you like your icing!

Directions: In the bowl of an electric mixer, blend together the cream cheese, butter and extracts. Gradually add enough confectioners' sugar to desired consistency and smooth. Frost cooled cupcakes and sprinkle generously with shredded unsweetened coconut.

White Hot Chocolate

(serves 8 to 10) Makes 9 cups.

4 c	whole milk	1 lb.	white chocolate, chopped
4 c	half-and-half	2 t	vanilla extract

Directions: In a medium saucepan, heat the milk and half-and-half to just below the simmering point. Remove the pan from the heat and add the white chocolate. When the chocolate is melted, add the vanilla and whisk to blend. Reheat gently and serve.

About the Author

Meredith Henning is an Economics graduate of Seattle University and lives with her family in Seattle Washington. She has home educated her four children for the past twelve years and counting, and she finds it a privilege and a joy to be part of their educational upbringing and faith formation. She may be found online at www.happyheartsmom.typepad.com where she blogs at Sweetness and Light about homeschooling, family life and love and faith. Mondays with Mary is her first book.

Lovely Lady Dressed in Blue

By Mary Dixon Thayer (1896)

Lovely Lady dressed in blue
Teach me how to pray!
God was just your little boy,
Tell me what to say!

Did you lift Him up, sometimes,
Gently on your knee?
Did you sing to Him the way
Mother does to me?

Did you hold His hand at night?
Did you ever try
Telling stories of the world?
O! And did He cry?

Do you really think He cares
If I tell Him things
Little things that happen? And
Do the Angels' wings

Make a noise? And can He hear
Me if I speak low?
Does He understand me now?
Tell me, for you know.

Lovely Lady dressed in blue
Teach me how to pray!
God was just your little boy,
And you know the way.